O Joy that sleekest me through pain,
I cannot close my heart to thee,
I trace the rainbow through the pain
And feel the promise is not vain
That morn shall tearless be.

—George Matheson, "O Love That Will Not Let Me Go", verse 3

JULIAN OF NORWICH

- APOSTLE OF PAIN

RICHARD NORTON

Richard Norton.

St. Cornelius the Centurion. 4 Feb. 2021.

authorHOUSE

AuthorHouse™ UK
1663 Liberty Drive
Bloomington, IN 47403 USA
www.authorhouse.co.uk
Phone: UK TFN: 0800 0148641 (Toll Free inside the UK)
UK Local: 02036 956322 (+44 20 3695 6322 from outside the UK)

© 2013 Richard Norton. All rights reserved.

No part of this book may be reproduced, stored in a retrieval system, or transmitted by any means without the written permission of the author.

Published by AuthorHouse 09/24/2020

ISBN: 978-1-6655-8058-8 (sc)
ISBN: 978-1-6655-8059-5 (hc)
ISBN: 978-1-6655-8060-1 (e)

Print information available on the last page.

Any people depicted in stock imagery provided by Getty Images are models, and such images are being used for illustrative purposes only.
Certain stock imagery © Getty Images.

This book is printed on acid-free paper.

Because of the dynamic nature of the Internet, any web addresses or links contained in this book may have changed since publication and may no longer be valid. The views expressed in this work are solely those of the author and do not necessarily reflect the views of the publisher, and the publisher hereby disclaims any responsibility for them.

Scripture quotations marked NKJV are taken from the New King James Version. Copyright © 1982 by Thomas Nelson, Inc. Used by permission. All rights reserved.

About the Author

Richard Norton has taught theology, philosophy, and church history in public schools, colleges, and universities in the UK, Sudan, and Zimbabwe. He has given keynote addresses on medieval Christian mysticism to gatherings of international scholars in the UK, Ireland, the United States, and Canada.

He is a member of a many learned societies, including the Royal Society of Arts, and has a great deal of involvement with the Julian Centre in Norwich.

Richard is a licensed lay reader in the Diocese of Gloucester, serving in the nine parish churches in Stroud. He has a keen interest in developing lay spirituality, prayer, and discipleship. He is married to Jacinta, also a theologian, to whom this book is dedicated. They have been married for over thirty years.

For Jacinta.
Scholar, teacher, wife, and friend.

Contents

Preface xiii
Acknowledgements..xv
Introduction xix

Chapter 1 Explanations, Interpretations, and Understandings... 1
              The Hermeneutical Arc of Paul Ricoeur................. 1
              Distanciation.. 3
              Appropriation... 7
              Level 1: What the Text Says 11
              Level 2: What the Text Is (Really) About 12
              Level 3: Text and the Lived Experience 13
              Conclusion 14
Chapter 2 Pain and the Imitatio Christi before Julian............17
              All in the Mind? Pain in the Medieval Intellectual
              Landscape 18
              The Experience of Pain 20

	Painful Effects... 23
	The Human Jesus and the Imitatio Chrisiti.......... 26
	Conclusion 49
Chapter 3	Julian of Norwich: Apostle of Pain 53
	Julian's Illness and the Showings 53
	Showings Seven and Eight: An Analysis131 58
Chapter 4	Explaining, Interpreting, and Understanding
	Julian's Spiritual Transformation through Pain..... 67
	The Level of Experience 69
	The Textual Level 75
Chapter 5	Closing Thoughts... 79

Appendix 83
Appendix Notes 95
Endnotes 97

Preface

This book explores the manifestations and understandings of pain in the Western medieval Christian tradition. It especially concerns the female theologian and mystic Julian of Norwich (ca. 1342–1416?). It is well-known that during a near fatal illness in the spring of 1373, God granted Julian sixteen "Showings" of his passion and crucifixion, as well as the all-embracing grace, mercy, and love which flow from them to every part of creation. She recorded her reflections on them almost immediately, and this has become known as the "Short Text". During the next twenty years, Julian prayerfully pondered the Showings and their wider theological and ethical implications for the wider Church. She produced the "Long Text" while living in the anchor hold attached to St Julian's Church in Norwich—hence her name.

English Christians had long been fascinated by the pain and wounds that Jesus received during his crucifixion, and they saw in them their own endurance of physical pain and suffering as a sharing in his passion. To do so, especially when that pain could hardly be borne, was to imitate Christ's suffering, or *imitatio Christi*. This may seem rather odd to twenty-first-century Christians, who may well regard it as being as spiritually and mentally unhealthy as it is unnecessary. But our near ancestors did not. The desire to suffer with Christ on the cross was motivated by a deep spiritual longing to be identified and united with God in Christ, reconciling the world to himself. Paradoxically, this made their suffering joyful and "sweet".

This book details those motivations and that paradox through an analysis of the seventh and eighth Showings to Julian. It tries to understand how both the tension between spiritual and physical experience and the apparent opposition between the unpleasant and the joyful might be explained. In doing so, it will employ the hermeneutic of phenomenology as found in Paul Ricoeur's notion of the "hermeneutical arc" of understanding. This means that to read Julian's texts is to understand them as the climax of Julian's own spiritual quest, moving as they do from a somewhat naïve to a deep understanding of her own experiences, from her own self to God. This book will argue that that movement was a dying and a rising. Through her own *imitatio Christi*, Julian died a spiritual death to her former self and rose to a rebirth of a new, enlightened, more compassionate and centred self, and so she becomes for us the Apostle of Pain.

Acknowledgements

We are all born into textual communities. Texts, of course, are far more than the words you are reading now. They are thoughts spoken and unspoken, colours, emotions, images, gestures, places, sensations, silences, smells, musical and cacophonous sounds, textures—anything and everything that forms us as the people we are and the people we might become.

So it is that this book, like all books, is palimpsest, containing many levels of meanings and the traces of the people who influenced its conception and helped to bring it to being. Some, but by no means all, of these people are as follows.

Rev Fr Gavin Berriman, Vicar of St Augustine's Parish Church Grove Park, South London, who first introduced me to all things Julian and who suggested that I read the Showings as *lectio divina* when I was greatly in need of the maternal love of God during a time of spiritual and personal crises.

Rev Kate Stacey, Rector of Stroud, for her enthusiasm for

embedding the contemplative tradition in the nine churches in her care, and for her wisdom as to how contemplation aids active discipleship in our communities as they grow together. Her continued support for both my ministry and my interest in Julian is ineffably valuable.

Rev Simon Howells, Pioneer Minister in Stroud, for his direction of the Center for Peace and the Arts and his conviction that the contemplative tradition binds people of all faiths and that as such it may be a useful tool in interfaith dialogue. I hope that what follows here may be a very small contribution to his work in this field.

Mr Barrie Voyce, Director of Illuminate, the youth ministry initiative throughout the Diocese of Gloucester. Although we are former colleagues working in a local Christian charity unlocking potential and offering opportunities for young people and their families, we are and will forever remain first and foremost brothers in Christ.

The congregations in Stroud, for whom I have a special care at the Church of the Holy Spirit Paganhill, St Paul's Whiteshill, and St John the Baptist Randwick. You continue to teach me far more than I can ever aspire to teach you.

Mr John Corkery at the University of Hertfordshire. Our ever-deepening bond of friendship runs over forty-five years since we were both young men gadding about town. Although we have sometimes vigorously disagreed about various matters, we have always mutually supported each other's quite different academic endeavours. In some ways I owe him more than he will ever know, and it is a pleasure to record that debt here.

The members of the Friends and Companions of Julian of Norwich, both in the UK and elsewhere, who have helped me reflect upon my way of life in the light of the Showings and who have encouraged not just my academic interest in Julian but also my spiritual devotion to her. The conversations I have had with many, particularly Howard Green (secretary) and Fr Luke Penket CJN (librarian and archivist), in the process of researching and writing this book has been invaluable. Fr Luke's insights are recorded in the appropriate endnotes. I continue to be grateful for having been given the opportunity to address the annual meeting in May 2019. All Friends and Companions continue to show that in their prayers and rule of life generally that "the strong have something to strive for and the weak nothing to run from" (Rule of St Benedict 64:19).

Members of my family, both living and dead. Although some have been at times a little sceptical as to the value of the mystical tradition in the modern world, nevertheless all believe that Christian love is the fundamental rule applicable to everyone, and they embed this in their daily living. Our discussions have helped clarify my thoughts on some difficult problems, but above all they are the cradle of my faith.

My companions, friends, mentors, and colleagues who do not always understand what I do or why I want to do it but who continue to believe that somehow it will come out all right in the end!

To my editor and publishers at AuthorHouse who have managed the "pregnancy" of this book so smoothly, patiently, and encouragingly from its conception to marketing. If any faults remain—and there are bound to be many—they are entirely mine.

My little white cat Minka, who has walked across this keyboard more times than enough, sometimes causing the need for a wholescale rewriting, but who nevertheless has been snuggled up nearby throughout always finding the sunniest spot.

And finally but by no means least (Matt 20:16), my wife of more than thirty years, Jacinta, to whom this book is dedicated. Her love, care, and critiques are always showings of divine as well as human love.

Introduction

The English Church of the Middle Ages was replete with images and different forms of spiritual writing concerned with human pain, suffering and death, and especially that of Jesus Christ in his passion and execution on a Roman cross. All of these were designed to produce ever deeper devotion and discipleship in individuals and whole congregations across the land. Many of these images and texts were lost during the Protestant insurgency, but similar images may still be seen in the churches and cathedrals of Spain, which contain statues portraying the beaten and bloody "Christ at the Pillar" or the post *rigour mortis* body of Jesus in numerous pietas. The written texts largely concerned semi-autobiographical accounts of visions, or journals recording moments of ecstatic prayer, spiritual marriage with Jesus, and other strange and often ineffable phenomena. Images, texts, and experiences were all highly charged spiritual encounters with God.

Nevertheless, although these encounters were what some

might call out-of-body, ethereal, and even imaginary experiences, the medieval texts often describe them as highly physical and involving real and intense physical pain and suffering. The pain is overwhelming. It must be fought against and rejected. Yet at the same time it is described as something joyous and sweet. This paradoxical duality is often one of central characteristics of medieval devotional works. One very good way of understanding this paradox is to take a long look at the way physical wounds and pain were understood in the medieval church.

This also provides a framework or context in which Julian's theology can be set before any analysis of the seventh and eighth Showings takes place.

For us, such writings, including those of Julian, are grouped together as "mystical" writings, or "mysticism", though the medieval authors themselves would not have understood the term because it is of relatively recent date. This recent grouping needs to be explained, so it is necessary to define some terms. What exactly do we mean by "mysticism" or "mystical experiences"? What, if anything, is common to these images and writings, which allows us to group them together under one head? In what ways and why is the experience of physical pain necessary for Julian's personal *imitatio Christi* and her final goal of union with God without loss of identity for either party? How do Julian's painful experiences contribute to her spiritual development—and to ours? How, if at all, may the tension between the physical and the spiritual on the one hand and the unpleasant yet sweet on the other hand be explained phenomenologically?

Once we have found some workable answers, we can then

undertake an analysis of Julian's Showings of Divine Love using a particular hermeneutic to read them; in this case, that of phenomenology, as we have it in the concept of the "hermeneutical arch" in the writings of Paul Ricoeur. This is a useful tool by which we can understand the ethical, spiritual, theological, and ecclesial implications of Julian's quest towards union with God via an *imitation Christi*. It works on two levels: first, as a reading of Julian's Showings as a personal quest in which Showings seven and eight mark her experiential climax, and second, on a textual level. I will briefly outline the theological development from the Short Text to the Long Text during the twenty years or so between the composition of the two manuscripts. By bringing both hermeneutical levels together by way of the cornerstone of the arch, I will argue throughout the book that Julian's objects of interpretation are the visions and experiences themselves. The text of the Showings contains its own lived interpretation. Moreover, Ricoeur's emphasis on the subject's appropriation is especially important for this book in view of the complex material that we will encounter. It allows for a reading of how Julian's own experiences and her interpretation of them points and moves towards a single *telos*, which is precisely the appropriation of her own experiences.

Julian's mystical experiences appeared to her in sixteen separate Showings, or Revelations, she received during a near fatal illness in May 1373. She recovered from her illness and subsequently wrote about them, as I stated in the preface, in what are now known as the Short and Long Texts. It is the Long Text which will form the primary text for much of this book.

A whole theological industry has arisen around Julian of Norwich in the last twenty years or so, and many of its products have helped many people (academic, ordained, or lay) to understand Julian's theology of love and the idea of God as Mother. Tragically, even these now familiar understandings are still regarded by some as both blasphemous and heretical. But Julian's theodicy, her theology of pain and suffering, has largely been neglected, and its relevance to us in the circumstances of the twenty-first century has therefore been overlooked.

This book is one attempt to fill that gap by way of an exploration of the medieval concept of pain in relation to *imitatio Christi*. This recurring theme has been insufficiently connected to Julian's experiences of "ecstatic pain". To do so now will, I hope, shed new light on Julian's Showings of Divine Love and, in so far as it is possible to do so, on the person of Julian herself.

CHAPTER 1

EXPLANATIONS, INTERPRETATIONS, AND UNDERSTANDINGS

The Hermeneutical Arc of Paul Ricoeur

In order to systematically understand the themes in Julian's writing which we will consider in later chapters, as well as their implications for us today, we need a theory of interpretation. We need, in the jargon, a hermeneutic. The one I have chosen here, because I believe it to be most appropriate to the material under consideration, is that of Paul Ricoeur.

The word "hermeneutic" derives from the Greek mythological figure Hermes, a messenger whose job it was to fly amongst the many gods of the Greek pantheon, delivering messages from Zeus (the father of all gods) and more especially interpreting them.[1] For our present purposes, I define hermeneutics as the site of what Ricoeur calls the "conflict of interpretations and the problem of dominations of interpretations". Ricoeur begins with the claim that interpretation is only possible because of the necessary divide between subjective intentions and meanings on the part of the author and its objective significance; that is, what the statements mean to others. Interpretation fills the gap between what the author intended to convey and what is understood in the mind of the reader—and this process is, of course, going on right here and right now as you read this. It occurs in every conversation too. That is why we speak so readily of having "misunderstood what you meant", or we say, "I just don't get what you're going on about."

The hermeneutical process can be said to begin when dialogue ends, because when we apply our minds to what we have just heard or read, further clarification comes. Without dialogue, we are forced to make an interpretation without the benefit of the other.[2] Ricoeur sought to explicate an epistemology of interpretation.[3] He focussed on textual interpretation as the primary aim of hermeneutics and developed a theory of interpretation which included language, reflection, and self-understanding.[4] Building on the questions posed by Heidegger, "What kind of being is it whose being consisted of understanding?" and Gadamer, "How is understanding possible in being?" Ricoeur asked, "Through what means is textual understanding possible?" In this endeavour, he tried to reunite truth, the characteristic of understanding, with the method, the operation through which understanding occurs. He also attempted to graft the traditional function of hermeneutics onto contemporary ontological insights. He wrote, for example, that interpretation was caught inside a circle formed by the conjunction of interpretation and interpreter.[5] The circle unites the gap of "distanciation".

Distanciation

Philosophically, distanciation—the putting of something at a distance—has its roots in the thought of Hans-Georg Gadamer and his hermeneutical principles that understanding arises from an awareness that all texts are situated in and influenced by a particular context, a history. Gadamer also states that understanding occurs when two horizons fuse, that of the author or speaker with that of the reader or listener. Fundamental to Ricoeur's theory is his understanding of text and especially his concept of distanciation: a standing separate from or being objective in relation to a text. Of itself, this tells us nothing about what Ricoeur thought a text is, but in *Hermeneutics and the Human Sciences*, he says that a text is "discourse fixed in writing".[6] Elsewhere, Ricoeur insisted that in his view, a text defined in this way displays "a fundamental characteristic of the historicity of human experience, namely that it is communication in and through distance".[7] He organised his discussion of this concept around four themes: first, a text as a relation of speech to writing; second, text as a structured work; third, text as the projection of a world; and fourth, text as a mediation of self-understanding.[8]

Ricoeur's discussion of the nature of the relationship between speech and writing rests on a parallel with the relationship between participants in a spoken discourse, which leads him to conclude that the distancing of text from the oral situation causes a change in the relationship between language and subjective concerns of both the author and the reader. He points out that in the case of speech, those who are involved in the discourse are present both with (in the psychological circumstances of the dialogue) and to each other (conscious of the non-verbal aspects of the dialogue). This is no longer achieved when the text takes the place of "live" discourse.

Ricoeur endeavoured to make clear which traits of discourse are altered by the passage from speech to writing. He argued that discourse, being an event occurring in a single point in time (history), is not preserved entirely unchanged when committed to written form such as articles or interview transcripts. He also pointed out that discourse refers to the speaker. It has a "world" (the world of discourse, its own context) and an "other", a hearer to whom it is addressed.

A discourse committed to text no longer necessarily coincides with what the author intended to say; the language they use, even in live discourse, does not necessarily convey to the listener what they intended to say. That is even more likely when discourse has become text and, for our purposes here, when a text such as Julian's Showings is not contemporary with current readers. This is because it now has a very different audience so that the audience itself is distanced from the social, psychological, or theological context of the original intended audience.[9]

The second theme of Ricoeur's discussion of distanciation is that of discourse as a work. He identified three distinctive traits of the notion of a work. First, a work is a sequence longer than a sentence. Second, a work is submitted to a form of codification. It has a literary genre. Both author and reader have some idea of what kind of writing it is that has been written and read. It is not possible to confuse, say, a statistical paper on the number of drug deaths in the UK with a sonnet.

Third, not only does a work sit within a genre, but it also has a specific literary style that relates to an individual. Again, it is not possible to confuse, say, Julian's Showings with *The Tin Drum* by Gunter Grass.[10] Ricoeur insisted that distanciation of discourse in the structure of a work does not obscure the fundamental purpose of the discourse, which is "someone saying something to someone[11] about something".[12]

This leads to Ricoeur's third modality of distanciation, namely text as the projection of a "world", which he calls the "world of text".[13] Live discourse always expresses the world, but it does this in the context of a reference or a reality that is common to the speaker and the audience—for example, how a listener might understand and react to the contents of the six o'clock news from the BBC. At this point, Ricoeur's theory is little different from that of Martin Heidegger's hermeneutical circle, in that the interpreter's inner world meets the unique world of each text to create a new picture or understanding of a possible world in the consciousness of the interpreter.

The fourth modality of distanciation, which Ricoeur regarded as the most fundamental, is what he called the "distanciation of the subject [the receiver of the discourse] from himself"[14] If we are to take seriously the distanciation by writing and by the structure of the work, as discussed above, then we can no longer, as Ricoeur has suggested, hold to the notion that understanding is a grappling of an alien life expressing itself through writing. Ricoeur's conclusion is that "in the last analysis the text is the mediation by which we understand ourselves". It is, as we will see in the specific case of Julian, self-appropriation.[15]

Through their foundation in language, texts stand on the boundary between the expressed and the unexpressed. For understanding to occur, both the expressed and the unexpressed require interpretation. Interpretation begins in a naïve way when the interpreter grasps the meaning of the entire text, after which the interpreter moves to a deeper understanding achieved through a recognition of the relationship of parts to the whole. Any naïve understanding means that the interpreter has already begun to formulate at least a rudimentary schema or explanation for meaning, which may or may not be confirmed as interpretation proceeds. In this way, interpretative understanding goes forward in stages; for Ricoeur, it is rising and circling to form an arch with continually reinforced links between the parts and the whole. These allow understanding to be changed, enlarged, and deepened. This dialectic between understanding and interpretation also allows us to see that repeated engagement with a text is necessary if premature interpretive closure is to be avoided. In the case of a text which is growing ever older, such as Julian's *Showings*, this process must be repeated again and again if we are to avoid the *reductio ad absurdum* too often applied to her writing in such a way that readers learn only that she said some things about everything turning out all right, that hazelnuts are theologically important, and that God has a feminine side.

Deeper understanding of a text requires time energy and patience if the initial naïve interpretation is to receive an opportunity for enlightenment of both the text and the self. [16] It means moving beyond understanding what a text seems to say to what the author really meant to convey. For Ricoeur, this has two stages which form the bedrock of his arch; first, an explanation of what a text says, and second, understanding what a text is properly about. Explanation is directed towards analysis of the internal relations of the self (the parts), whereas understanding is directed towards grasping the meanings the text discloses (the whole in relation to the parts). Only in this way can what Ricoeur calls "appropriation" come about.

Appropriation

Philosophically appropriation (making something one's own), like distanciation, has its modern roots in the work of Hans-Georg Gadamer and his concept of tradition. For Gadamer, tradition consists in a shared history and an acknowledged dominant intellectual and material culture. It is essential that these are in place as a means of binding communities and nations together if that community or nation is to have a distinct identity and if meaning and understanding are to be shared. These things prefigure understanding. Through participation in the tradition in which we live, we gain a sense of having a place of safety, a sense of belonging with others, so that together we can empower and equip each other to face the rigours and pleasures of life and create a shared optimism for a hopeful future. Tradition, then, is not something stuffy, belonging only to a conventional past with fixed norms and expected patterns of behaviour which might make it quite alien to how we live now. Rather, it is something into which we have grown and will continue to grow so long as we are alive. It is something we have appropriated through engaged living.

Appropriation of textual meaning is the same. When interpreters appropriate the meaning of a text, it is no longer alien and becomes familiar. Indeed, a text from hundreds of years ago, like Julian's Showings, can become so familiar and loveable for us that the years roll away so that for all practical, theological, and spiritual purposes, it is as if her words are spoken to us directly by one of our contemporaries. Her traditional words and insights are alive through our engaged living with her text.

Accordingly, appropriation and distanciation provide a dialectic of interpretation between the now and long ago, the near and far away, the familiar and the unfamiliar, the known and the unknown or foreign. This conceptualisation related well to the view that interpretative scholarly research into, say, the writings and world of Julian of Norwich strives to reveal the hidden, unknown, alien, or fragmented within a tradition and thus appropriately meets the needs of interpretative researchers.

Methodologically, interpretation allows actualisation of the meanings of a text, and for Ricoeur this occurs through appropriation, making one's own.[17] What is made one's own is the world of the text, and as a result, the horizon of the interpreter (one's knowledge or self-awareness) is expanded. Thus, interpretation is the process through which disclosure of new modes of being "gives to the interpreter a new capacity of knowing himself."[18] In this way, interpretative understanding opens up the possibility of seeing things differently and of orientating ourselves to the world in other ways. This link between lived experience, understanding, and self-awareness grounds Ricoeur's hermeneutical theory of interpretation in daily life. It takes account of being and the relation of being with others so that every hermeneutics is explicitly or implicitly self-understanding by means of understanding others, such as a text.[19]

This renewed understanding of self allows a return to the text with a newly expanded horizon from which to understand it. It also highlights the intersubjective nature of interpretive findings and the need for interpreters not to project themselves into a text—a reading back. Indeed, appropriation is not an act of conquest whereby we possess a text; rather, it is a moment of dispossession of our narcissistic ego. In the degree to which appropriation might be thought of as any kind of possession, the interpreter and the text itself mutually captivate one another. The opportunity for greater and deeper interpretations resides in the space created by the dispossession of the ego; these opportunities are for the text to reveal its worlds.[20]

Together, the aspects of Ricoeur's theory discussed so far form the paradigm of textual interpretation. Of most significance is that this is a fresh approach to the relationship between explanation and interpretation, the unfolding of which involves the movement back and forth between the parts of the text and a view of the whole, during the process of interpretation. Ricoeur used the term "hermeneutical arc" to describe this movement back and forth between a naïve understanding and an in-depth interpretation. The arc is characterised by movement back and forth between the world of text and a new understanding of the world of discourse. In coming to the term "hermeneutical arc", Ricoeur did not discount the hermeneutical circle proposed by Heidegger, but placed even more emphasis on the correlation between explanation and understanding.

Ricoeur indicated that there are two ways of looking at a text. The first of these he described as considering only the internal nature of the text. From this perspective, it has no context and no external world, and there is no consideration of it having had an author and audience: "based on this choice, the text has no outside, but only an inside, it has no transcendent aim".[21] What arises from it in this case is the explanation which is only possible with the objectivity of the text (distanciation), which I have discussed above. At this level, understanding is quite immature. It includes, for example, the meaning of the words "as the reader understands them", which may or may not be congruent with the meaning the author intended to convey.

Ricoeur's proposed second way of looking at a text is to restore it to a living communication with a proper place in tradition, as defined in the ways we have also looked at a little while ago. Through interpretation, the world of the text combines with the world of the reader to form something entirely new. At first, this interpretation is still superficial and unsubstantial. However, as readers continue to explore the text, they begin to take into account a number of other factors. These factors are open to amendment and perhaps wholesale change. Where they are in error, they must be discarded so that a new and correct understandings can take their place, and so interpretation changes and grows. Ricoeur summarised this thus: "To explain is to bring out the structure, that is, the internal relations of dependence, which constitute the statics of the text, to interpret is to follow the path opened up by the text, to place oneself on route toward the orient of the text."[22]

Ricoeur's route takes place on at least three levels, all of which will be revisited in a later chapter when I will directly apply them to Julian's writing.

Level 1: What the Text Says

Ricoeur boldly states, "The choice in favour of meaning is the main presupposition of any hermeneutics."[23] To choose meaning necessitates interpretation.[24] However, words and phrases are polysemic because they invoke as many meanings as there are to be found in them. This can create an almost impossible situation for a reader of any text and one that can only be overcome by "pinning down" the meaning, if only temporarily. Discourse allows us to demarcate the apparently endless possibilities by setting a context in which words are used and, by doing so, momentarily truncate the play of meanings. The process of reading is constitutive of the production of meaning as the two poles dialectically play into the structure of a text.[25]

At this stage, readers faced with a text need to follow an answer to a question: What does the text say? In the process of explanation, readers understand only naïve meanings of words and phrases, and they only fully understand part of what they are reading. From this perspective, the text does not establish any connection between author and reader, the world of a text and the reader's lived experience. As noted earlier, only the outside of the text appears at this stage. The inside is entirely absent.

If we take an example of a lecturer and her students, it is important that they do not answer the question together. Rather, the students must think about it for themselves and try to focus their thoughts in ways which will extract apparent meaning of words and the basic meaning of the text in view. At this level, the main emphasis on the text's internal communication lies only with the student's own world, if at all.[26]

Level 2: What the Text Is (Really) About

Perhaps the central way in which we reveal our unique being and personality to the world is through our engagement with it through work. Through work there is a high degree of interaction between ourselves as subjects and the objects we observe and manipulate. We look around us and observe ourselves in our work, our discourse as work. Again, educators are no strangers to this notion. Many a classroom, from nursery to secondary level, is decorated with the work pupils have done. Their work reveals how each pupil uniquely attempts to understand the world. However, before working in the world, we must reckon with being in the world, which foregrounds our comprehension of it. Our being in the world always precedes our reflection on the world. It excludes the possibility of complete and total reflection because we must first understand the meaning before we can try to transform it through language and social practice.[27]

At this second level, then, the reader of a text must ask, "What is the text talking about?" At this level, Ricoeur suggests that readers answer that question in ways which help them understand the text and which will restore the text to the reader's world. It is in this way that readers will build on their initial understanding and start to discover more of the text through slow reflection and rumination upon it. Theologically, this is akin to the practice of *lectio divina*. According to Ricoeur this slow rumination is essential if the horizons of the reader and the author are to meet; indeed, it is central to the whole hermeneutical approach. According to this view, data are, as it were, imposed, but understanding cannot be imposed because understanding must and can only be achieved within a person.[28]

Level 3: Text and the Lived Experience

Following the work of existentialist philosophers and Martin Heiddegger in particular, Ricoeur explains that human beings are alone and "inauthentic" for most of our lives. We are "thrown" into a world as beings, which puts responsibility of understanding our situation firmly and squarely on our shoulders and promotes distance from others. However, we also exist in the world with others that we are "condemned to interpret" and appropriate.[29]

As a dialogical structure, appropriation or being together overcomes our fundamental distance of being alone.[30] So it is that we always exist in a world with others, and the challenge is to acknowledge this precondition. This is partly accomplished through discourse with other human beings, which is why hermeneutics is the first understanding of a world projected by discourse (a mother talking to her new baby), the kind of world it offers. It is ultimately that which distinguishes human beings from the animal kingdom: "Only man has a world and not just a situation."[31]

Through interpretations, we understand not only a psychological subject but an existential project in the Heideggerian sense. At least for the moment, discourse struggles against the alienation brought about by our existential condition. Similarly, even before we can reflect on our conditions, we must understand our being in the world, a belonging which precedes any thought about itself—in Ricoeur's words, the "power to be".[32]

At this third level, the understandings gained in the previous levels are now applied to the reality of life. We link our understandings to the world in such a rational way that the text interprets the world of lived experience and vice versa; horizons meet. The inner and the outer world collide and fuse, becoming one in a continually deepening dialogue, until we reach at least a modicum of "authenticity".[33]

Conclusion

In this chapter, I have summarised Ricoeur's 1981 theory of interpretation. I have affirmed the basic insights of his method and philosophy and outlined the building blocks of his hermeneutical arc, the understanding of texts through distanciation, appropriation, and the three levels considered above.

The building block of Ricoeur's arc will be important in a later chapter in which I apply them to the ways in which Julian of Norwich was transformed by her Showings, not least in her appropriation of them.

CHAPTER 2

PAIN AND THE IMITATIO CHRISTI BEFORE JULIAN

This chapter charts the devotion to the wounds of Christ during the eleventh and twelfth centuries. It will note some of the paradigmatic shifts in thinking in these centuries before Julian because, as we will see later, they form a background against which her own writing is set, and she responds to them in both positive and negative ways.[34] Devotional practices moved from thoughtful rumination on the wounds of Christ to powerful and emotive mysticism.

All in the Mind? Pain in the Medieval Intellectual Landscape

In this section, I aim to show how medieval writers approached the mind-body problem, highlighting some key areas in which their ideas were particularly relevant to their thinking about pain—a psychology of pain—set in a unique intellectual landscape. It is important to look closely at this landscape if we are to properly consider how our medieval ancestors wrote about their lived experience of pain.

The landscape has many of its roots in the doctrine of the four humours begun by Hippocrates and developed by Galen. This doctrine underpinned the notion of a mind-body continuum because humours shaped thinking about both mind and body. The distinction between mind and body was, in some ways, far more complex and fluid than our current thinking on the point, which is largely derived from Cartesian dualism and its development during the Enlightenment and the rise of so-called secularism. The medieval distinction was complicated by ideas of the soul, where in the body certain bodily functions were located, and the integration of thought and affect.

The term "mind", for example, originated with the concept of memory but quickly overlapped with notions of the soul, and it took on at least some aspects of what we would easily recognise as part of our contemporary definitions of mind. Aristotle situated the human capacity for reason and intellectual thought in the soul and regarded the heart as the centre of the senses and emotions, as the many romantics among continue to do. By contrast, Galen believed that each of these things was a function of the brain. Neoplatonic philosophers situated the rational, immortal part of the soul in the head and the emotions and appetites in the trunk of the body. In the fourth century AD, St Augustine of Hippo saw the will as a faculty of the superior soul and associated emotions with the lower, inferior body even though he saw the emotions as having both cognitive and bodily aspects.[35]

Something akin to a recognisable modern psychology came into focus towards the end of the thirteenth century, about a hundred years or so before Julian received her Showings. This followed a rediscovery of the works of Aristotle in the twelfth century as a result of Arabic versions of his texts being translated into Latin. Thinkers of this period such as Avicenna, Thomas Aquinas, Albertus Magnus, and Roger Bacon developed theories of the mind based on this rediscovery and translations. They believed observations of the effects of head injuries had confirmed Galen's view that the rational aspects of the psyche were in the brain, though some persisted with the idea that both understanding and emotion were located in the heart. Cognition was believed to be a two-part process, with psychological mechanisms in the brain mirrored by processes in the mind or soul. Neither was reducible to the other.

The brain was instrumental in transforming the "vital spirit" (one part of a tripartite system of spirits derived from Arabic philosophy) into the "animal spirit", which controlled sensation, bodily movement, imagination, cognition, and memory. The main work was done by the cerebral ventricles, which housed the "inner senses", responsible for integrating external senses and constructing thoughts about them from their component concepts or "forms" (*imagines* or *phantasmata*), which were, in essence, an amended version of the Platonic idea of forms. Perception worked by the reception of sensory impressions in the anterior part of the brain (the *sensus communis*, or common sense) and their temporary storage in the imagination or working memory. Those impressions were then passed on for creative shaping in the middle part of the brain, the imaginative (*phantasy*) where yet another area of the brain, known as the estimative, took over and began to get to work on memory-based and emotionally coloured judgements. Finally, these were passed to the back part of the brain, the *cellula memoralis,* the storehouse of the fully formed memory.

The *phantasmata* that resulted from this complex process were not abstract concepts alone. They were saturated by sensory qualities and were emotionally charged.

The Experience of Pain

Historical attitudes to the lived experience pain have only relatively recently begun to receive scholarly attention. Perhaps one of the first to enter this field was Phillip Ziegler's *The Black Death*.[36] But his was largely an epidemiological study of the transmission of the disease and its subsequent effects on society, economy, and ecclesiastical thinking rather than one which dealt with how an individual experienced, in the body, the three types of plague. More recently, Jack Hartnell has discussed the medieval understanding of medieval bodies, but again, he did so through a contribution to the history of art.[37] Both Laura A. Fink and Ellen

Ross have persuasively written on the relation of medieval female bodies and visions granted to women.[38] Some ten years later, Ester Cohen produced her magisterial work *The Modulated Scream*.[39]

Cohen argues that although pain remains the same in every era, the uses, expressions of, responses to, and attitudes towards pain vary considerably over time. She claims that her book is not about pain "because pain itself cannot be known".[40] Rather, it is a book about how people thought about pain; how they conceptualised it, explained it to themselves and to others; and what they did in order to find relief.[41] Cohen had earlier argued elsewhere that until "little over a century ago, pain was accepted as a given. It could, if necessary be eased by various means, but nobody really saw any reason to try to eradicate it in any and all painful situations".[42] Thus, the alleviation of pain for the sake of ridding oneself of an evil that should be vanquished seems to be a relatively modern phenomenon arising, perhaps, with aseptic surgical methods. "Perhaps the greatest revolution in western attitudes towards pain," Cohen wrote, "is the transition from attempts at controlling pain to attempts to controlling sensation."[43]

In modern Western society, pain is unnatural and opposed to an expectation of comfort. Should pain arise, we swallow a painkiller or consult a doctor. We want pain to be suppressed and controlled as quickly as possible and by the most efficient means. Better still, pain should be for as brief a period as possible because we think pain is harmful by reason of the thing it is. To say the very least, pain is always unpleasant. In other words, modern Western society places an independent value on freedom from pain.

Although it is extremely difficult to find good and satisfactory definitions of pain, we all have in common a lived experience of what pain feels like. It is often difficult to describe, and the more intense the pain, the more it seems to elude our descriptions. Neurologists, biomedical scholars, and others have tried to explain what happens in the brain of mystics when they have their transcendent or ecstatic experiences, especially where pain is felt at the same time. However, it is impossible to say for certain what goes on in the mystics' brain when they have their holy dreams and visions.

Historical accounts are full of descriptions and interpretations of other people's pain and behaviour as a result of their pain. The mystical writers wrote about their painful experiences and are thus highly important first-hand accounts of pain as an expression of compassion and suffering with Christ. When dealing with historical descriptions of pain, as with historical sources generally, we need to bear in mind that they are subjective accounts of painful experiences that need interpretation. When dealing with first-hand, autobiographical accounts, however, this is undoubtedly easier because we only have to interpret the actual account as the sufferer records it and not, for instance, second-hand accounts of pain in other people.

In this discussion of Julian's account of her ecstatic pain, I will apply concepts and ideas from the field of theology, philosophy, and phenomenology and examine them in the light of the medieval mystics' description of the experience of pain as being at once intensely hurtful and sweet and joyous. Then I will examine the significance of physical suffering for the idea of *imitatio Christi*.

Painful Effects

The role of physical pain in theology is unclear and has not received the systematic treatment we might expect. Large parts of the Bible suggest that pain is an evil, an absence of the good (*privatio boni*) which, because of its supposed links to sin, is something we want to be rid of.[44] Pain is never neutral because it is already affectively charged as unpleasant. Pain is unpleasant because it is something that should not be, and we cannot but help wish it away. What turns pain into suffering is surely the fact that once it has first occurred, it encapsulates the bodily experience, yet at the same time all we can do is wish the pain to go away, or for us to go away from the pain. Furthermore, not only do we experience pain through our bodies, but pain is the human experience that, to the highest possible extent, manifests human embodiment. Nothing makes us more self-conscious than when we experience physical pain, although we are not normally aware of our bodies and what we do with them when they function normally. When we experience physical pain, we become overwhelmingly focused on our bodies and our pain. It is as though when we are in pain, we no longer have bodies—we become nothing but a body.

This has been noted by Drew Leder in his book *The Absent Body*.[45] He takes as his starting point the peripatetic and later empiricist assumption that all human experience is rooted and grounded in and through the body: "nothing in the mind not first through the senses" (*Nihil est in intellectu quod non sit prius in sensu*). Despite this, we are not normally aware of its presence. Leder asks, "Why is the body so often absent from experience?"[46]

When the body functions normally, we are largely unaware of its functions, and we do not give a thought to the fact that we breathe or that our heart beats. Yet these functions are literally life-giving and vital to our survival. This unawareness is what Leder calls "the absent body". When everything is in order, the body is absent, and that enables us to engage with other matters. This is decisive in our ability to engage in the world around us. Leder refers to this as the "ecstatic body".[47] However, when the body fails to function normally, when we become ill, or when we feel physical pain, we become more aware of it. This is what Leder calls the "disappearing body".[48] The pain seizes the body and "Places upon the sufferer … an affective call".[49] He describes this call or seizure of pain in this way:

> I am seized by pain in a way I am not by other experiences of the body. I can choose to look in the mirror or not, to pay attention or not to my kinesthesias. Even strong pleasures, such as those of a sexual nature, may leave one's thoughts wandering. Aesthetic, objective, or pleasurable self- encounters retain a large volitional element. With pain this is less the case, not only because of its typically involuntary etiology but because of the quality of the sensation itself.[50]

The central object of our study here is Julian's bodily experience of pain. The idea of pain as an evil, a seething that should not be, presents a paradox in her mystical vision. Although her pain is excessive, it is also described in terms of positive affect; she both does and does not want her pain to go away. She has, after all, prayed for it and so rejoices in it. Indeed, her mystical experiences are enhanced and achieved precisely through her bodily pain such that it is quite impossible to think of her experience apart from her pain. They are inseparable, and it is this interconnectedness that leads her to that should not be but, on the contrary, had a purpose. It definitely should be, because it, like sin, is behovenly. This does not mean that Leder's insights cannot be applied to the medieval perception of pain because he addresses the experience of pain as something that turns the person who feels it towards her own body and self and centres the attention on the pain itself. This is precisely what Julian does.

I insist on a paradox that is not addressed by Leder—namely, the constructive meaning and positive affect of the pain, which I ultimately consider to be two sides of the same coin, as I will make clear in a later chapter. Despite this positive affect and meaning of the pain emphasised in the Middle Ages, however, the persistent idea that pain is a natural evil still holds. It is merely one aspect of the pain, but it a highly significant aspect. Were the pain not also unpleasant and aversive (given in Julian's case and bringing her to the gate of death), it would lose its purpose because it simply would not be pain at all.

Here, we encounter another paradox; precisely when we experience pain it, becomes impossible to forget ourselves. As Leder remarked, "Physical suffering constricts not only the spatial but the physical sphere. As it pulls us back to the *here,* so severe pain summons us to the *now.*"[51] How, then, is this compatible with a loss of self, the absent body? In a later chapter, I draw on these two observations—that physical pain leads to an intense experience of the here and now, and that the joyous aspect of pain simultaneously involves a loss of self—and argue that both are at play in Julian's visions. Moreover, I will argue that this tension and paradox finds resonance in the idea of *imitatio Chrisiti*.

The Human Jesus and the *Imitatio Chrisiti*

The term "Docetism" (from Greek, "to seem") refers to the early Christian but largely Gnostic view that Jesus only seemed to be a human being. According to this view, because he only seemed to be a human being but was not so in fact, Jesus was incapable of human suffering, and consequently his Passion was only an illusion. Although this view was officially condemned as heresy by the Council of Chalcedon in AD 451, the mystery of Christ's humanity was still a central problem that was widely discussed, contemplated, and written about throughout the Middle Ages. The general view was that although Christ was divine and thus immortal, he was also human and so voluntarily suffered the greatest possible pain. This was itself fully consistent with the Chalcedonian formula of the hypostatic union of the two natures: Jesus is both fully a person and fully God.

That God became the human being called Jesus means that God shares our human conditions. But why should pain serve as the touchstone for God's incarnation? Pain may serve as a touchstone because more than any other phenomenon, it proves how Jesus's person, his "I", is indissolubly connected to his body.

Christ's suffering on the cross defines him as incarnated and human, because pain is the primary human experience that manifests our corporeality. Because the pain is so essential for the definition of the human, incarnated Christ, it also becomes essential to the *imitatio Christi* through which Julian achieved union with the divine, the highest bliss and joy, and her telos (ultimate aim).

The idea of *imitatio Christi* evolved alongside, and perhaps even because of, this Christological idea of Jesus sharing human suffering "even to death on a cross".[52] The desire to identify with Christ and take a share in his suffering became a central idea for mystics, martyrs, saints, and ascetics, and as part of this aim, they prayed for and embraced physical pain. Because Christ had suffered pain, and not just seemingly, the pain of the mystics ideally had to be physical too. Apparent, illusionary pain (could such a thing exist) would not sufficiently imitate Christ's real and physical pain. Rather, it might suggest, one can imagine that Christ's pain was simply spiritual and "seeming" rather than real and physical. Thus, I argue it was essential that the suffering described by Julian and recorded in her visions was as real and as physical as she says it was and not some literary trope or framework against which to set her theology. When Julian experienced physical pain alongside and in her spiritual visions, she experienced a real *imitatio* and communion with Christ, both physically and spiritually.

As noted earlier, pain is the one human experience that expresses our corporeality to the highest degree. Following this, the physically manifested pain that Julian experienced is the closest possible she could get to the ideal of *imitatio Christi* as she perceived a union with Christ through her suffering. The body, with all its pain, was the channel through which she experienced her visions.

The foundational Biblical Text that forms the basis of the devotion through *imitatio Christi* was John 19:33–34, 37. The Orthodox Study Bible (which is largely a reiteration of the Vulgate) translates the original Greek as follows: "But when they came to Jesus and saw that he was already dead, they did not break his legs. But one of the soldiers *pierced his side* with a spear and immediately water and blood came out … And again another scripture says They shall look on Him whom they pierced."[53] This already allows us to sum up the paradigm shifts as a movement from devotion to the wounds in Christ's side to the wound in the heart.

It is useful to begin with the Venerable Bede for whom the wound described in the Vulgate text proved a rich source of metaphor and allegorical interpretation and formed the basis of a complete devotion ensemble. Only later, from the twelfth century to our own day, via Julian, was the text understood to mean that the spear pierced Christ's heart. What had been considered a wound that opened the interior of Christ's body so that fountains of sacramental grace welled up from it became a wound in his heart so that that the organ as a source of life and love poured forth its vital power on all humankind.

The symbolic power of the heart has always been a dominant theme in Western culture. The Old and New Testaments are full of references to the heart as the centre of both human and divine compassion.[54] But it is after the eleventh century that Christ's heart, purportedly opened by Longinus's lance, became the focus of his passion and the emblem of intense love and union with Christians.[55] It may come as a surprise to some Christians that the exegetical and iconographic topos of the Sacred Heart is historically late. There are three reasons for this delayed development: physiological, semantic, and affective.

First, the widespread patristic and non-canonical tradition that the lance pierced Christ's right side makes an entry of the lance into Christ's heart on the left side physiologically unlikely, although one physician has argued that it may be possible.[56] The idea that the lance pierced the right side may find support in the Ethiopic version of John's Gospel and is nearly universal in the art and iconography of the crucifixion.[57] But the physiological impediment was eventually ignored for the symbolic rectitude of right over left (dexter over sinister), and for typological analogies favouring the right side, such as water flowing from the right side of the temple, as in Ezekiel's vision.[58]

Second, the semantic problem. Neither in the text John 19:33–34 nor in the supporting text at John 7:37–38 does "heart" occur. In the latter text, the author of the Gospel quotes Jesus at the Feast of Tabernacles: "If anyone thirst, let him come [to me]; and let him drink who believes in me. As the scripture says, 'From within him shall flow rivers of living waters.'"[59] "Within him" can apparently be translated from the Greek for "the belly", not, despite modern translations, "from the heart".

Third, the delay in concentration on the heart as the seat of love. Origin, Ambrose, Augustine, and Bede treat the heart as the moral and spiritual core of the human being, quoting Christ's words: "Learn of me for I am meek and humble of *heart*" (Matt.

11:29).[60] Yet the concentration on Christ's heart as a seat of all-consuming love for all humankind is, I think, a distinguishing mark of Cistercian spirituality, and then of the religious orders of men and women from the twelfth century onwards.[61] Therefore the exegesis of the Johannine texts by the Fathers and early medieval commentators, such as Bede, remains on the wound in Christ's side and the cavity that the spear made in his interior, considered as a well from which poured forth his redeeming blood and sacral water. Only later did devotional writers, following the Cistercians, locate the wound in Christ's heart.

Adopting the interpretations of the Fathers, Bede saw the birth of the Church in Christ's sending out his spirit from the cross and the pouring out of blood and water from the wound in Christ's side. By Christ's passion and death, the sacramental water of baptism purifies, and the blood of the Eucharist redeems and nourishes. Drawing upon the comparisons of Augustine, Bede says that just as Eve came from the side of Adam while he was asleep, so the Church was formed during Christ's sleep of death.[62]

I think Bede is suggesting that in some curious way, the Church is both daughter and spouse, a trope familiar to him in the Song of Songs 4:9, "my sister, my bride". In a homily for Holy Week, Bede argued that the Church "has been produced from the side of the Redeemer, that is, imbued with the water of cleansing and the blood of sanctification when he was dying for her sake".[63] In his commentary on the First Epistle General of John, Bede points out that the living water and blood poured forth from the dead body of the Lord gave us life.[64] Here, Bede is emphasising a repetitive theme inherent in Johannine texts.

In a homily on Luke 24:36–47, Bede explained why the resurrected Jesus showed the wounds in his side to the disciples.

> It was not without cause that he ordered them to see and recognise the marks in his hands and feet instead of his countenance, which they knew equally well. He ordered it so that, when they saw the signs of the nails with which he had been fastened to the cross, they would be able to understand that it was not only a body which they saw, but the very body of the Lord, which they knew had been crucified. Hence John, when he mentions the appearance of the Lord, does well to testify that he also saw his disciples his side, which had been wounded by the soldier, so that as they recognised many indications of the passion they knew so well he had undergone, they might rejoice with more certain faith in the resurrection and the destruction of death he had accomplished.[65]

Bede then gave four reasons why the resurrected body of Jesus retained the marks of crucifixion: Jesus was not a spirit without a body but a spiritual body; by keeping the scars forever, he shows what he has done for all people for all time; they are an object of contemplation and thanksgiving for the faithful; and they are an object of shame to those who "pierced him" (John 19:37). For Bede, this is a central verse, and he looks forward to other parts of the New Testament and back to the Old Testament, taking great pains to draw other biblical passages into alignment with it. For example, in his Commentary of the Acts of the Apostles, Bede suggests that the incident at John 12:7, in which the angel struck Peter, is a reminder of the piercing of Jesus in the passion. For us today, these efforts may seem too exaggerated, and his interpretations may be more than a little forced, but his contemporaries would have noted that Bede was attempting to deal with the wounds of Jesus, especially the wound in the side, in two quite different ways.

In his commentaries on Mark, Luke, Acts, and the general Pastoral Epistles, he discusses the wounds in a simple and direct way. He relates them to passages in the Old Testament, which he thinks prefigure the Passion. He points out the spiritual significance of Jesus's wounds for faithful discipleship. But in doing all this, he does not stray too far into creating them into types or tropes, being content to show the irony that through Christ's wounding we are healed, just as by his death we have life.

In his commentaries on the Old Testament, specifically Genesis, Samuel, Ezra, and the Song of Songs, Bede does explore an elaborate allegorical hermeneutic. He becomes elusive and poetic. He alludes to Christ's wounds in a complex and figurative sense. He pushes both theological method and language to its limits.

How are we to explain these different approaches? It seems to me that the difference of treatment derives from what Bede saw as the function of the Old and New Testaments in the Christian community and especially the function of allegory and other tropes in the interpretation of them. Indeed, I think Bede is claiming to stand in a particular theological tradition which began with Origen and was more or less consistent throughout the whole patristic period: a tradition which understood the events, the people, and the descriptive details of the Old Testament as symbolically pregnant with meaning for the interpretation of the New Testament. In understanding the Old Testament, its allegorical meaning is far superior to its literal meaning. Bede made this explicitly clear in his remarks on the book of Tobit (which the Protestant Bible regards as apocryphal).

> Yet anyone who knows how to interpret the text not just historically but allegorically, sees that just as fruits surpass their leaves, this book's inner sense surpasses its literal simplicity. For if understood spiritually it is seen to contain ... the great mysteries of Christ and his Church.[66]

The Old Testament was a mine from which gems were to be extracted and polished to make the light of Christ in the New Testament shine ever more brightly. An example of this is the *Moralia* of Gregory the Great and his understanding of the Book of Job. The *Moralia* was a text almost certainly known to Bede, and it greatly influenced him. In short, for Bede as for Gregory, the Old Testament was not important in and for itself but only insofar as and in the degree to which it could be regarded as a portent of what was to come in the New Testament. It followed that, in contrast, the New Testament is inherently significant, a self-referential reality that fulfils and completes every Old Testament figure. The New Testament and the Church are the historical actualisation of what the allegory in the Old Testament presaged.

Bede's treatment of the wounds of Christ therefore varies according to whether he writes from the context of a passage or verse in the Old Testament, or whether he is working in the historical context of the New Testament and its sacramental meaning in the life of Christian women and men. For Bede, as for Origen and the Cappadocian Fathers and the Patristics, the Old Testament is allegorical, poetic, suggestive, and symbolic of a later reality, whereas the New Testament is non-relative and historically realised in the here and now.

A good example of this is the way in which Bede links Noah's Ark to the crucifixion. The open door of the Ark represents the wound in Christ's side. Both are vessels of salvation from the storms of destruction. Genesis 6:16 reads, "Now when you assemble the ark, you shall gradually finish it up to a cubit at the top and set the door down on it's side."

Bede says of this:

> This door through which entered both men and animals that were to be saved designates the very unity of faith, without which no one is able to enter ... "one Lord, one faith, one baptism." One God, for the door is aptly placed in the side, because it signifies that very large entry which was opened in the side of the Lord Saviour placed on the cross, from which "immediately flowed forth blood and water" (John 19:34). By those mysteries all of the

faithful are received into the one company of the Holy Church as into the interior of the ark. The entry is to be placed not only in the side ... but "down". This signifies the humility of the Lord himself through which he died for us, or our own, without which we are unable to be saved. Likewise, the entry into the ark is down and placed near the earth, so that there the men and animals to be saved would enter, and having entered they soon would ascend to the higher decks into their own places, because the Lord appearing in the depths of this mortality "was wounded on account of our iniquities", so that he might lead us redeemed through the mysteries of his wounds to the supernal seats of the virtues in the present life and by an invisible ascent to the supernal rewards in heaven.[67]

The wound in Christ's side allows Christians to enter the "many mansions" (John 14:2) prepared for them in heaven, just as Noah and his family found safety in rooms of the Ark.

The wood of the Ark prefigures the wood of the cross, even in its dimensions. The Ark was thirty cubits long, and the Greek letter for thirty is Tau, which takes the form of the cross. Even the human body has the same dimensions because the ideal body is Christ's.[68]

In his thirty questions on the Book of Kings, Bede begins to develop a metaphor based on the Temple. Christ is the embodiment of all that the Temple was (John 2:19), the incarnation of its symbolism in the life of individuals and for Israel as the people of God. The wound of the Passion in Christ's side is the door to the temple through which Christian disciples may pass from this earthly life and into the joys of heaven. According to Bede, just as the main entrance to the Temple in Jerusalem faced west and had a portal to the right that led directly into the cenaculum, or upper floors, so the crucified Christ faced westwards has the pierced entry in his side which leads to his more divine chambers, where faithful Christians can be cleansed by the waters of baptism and our spiritual thirst slaked by his most precious blood. Being thus refreshed in both our bodies and our souls, we know that we will be with him both now and at the final resurrection and united in him forever.[69]

Like many monastics of his day and later, Bede had a fondness for the Song of Songs, so it should not surprise us that even here, he saw symbolic references to the wounds and Passion of Christ. Indeed, for Bede the whole book prefigures just that. On the verse "Come my dove into the clefts of the rock, into the crannies of the wall" (Song of Songs 2:14), he says this:

> If, according to the exposition of the Apostle (Paul) "the rock was Christ" (1 Cor. 10:4), what are the clefts of the rock except the wounds that Christ received for our salvation? Indeed, in those clefts the dove resides and nests when the meek soul or indeed the whole church places its sole hope of salvation in the Lord's passion.[70]

From the time of Bede to the Conquest and on to Julian of Norwich in the fourteenth century, this sort of symbolism and the devotion to the wounds of Christ which arose from it was always strong in liturgy, in literature, in public and private prayer, and in art. Besides depictions of Christ's bleeding wounds in manuscript illustrations, Books of Hours, and sculpture, the piercing of Christ's side by the soldier's lance was singled out for special treatment[71] and even in architecture.[72] It was certainly central to the devotion and theology of St Bernard of Clairvaux (1090–1153) and the early Cistercians.

Bernard turns the image of the courtly lover into a fervent exponent of spiritual love. The chivalric love of the elusive lady becomes complete devotion to Christ while retaining its amatory, intensely personal, and even sensuous aspects. Christ's wounds are the ineffable marks of sacrificial love and the token of divine mercy.

> There is no lack of clefts by which his mercy is poured out. They pierced his hands and his feet. They gored his side with a lance, and through these fissures I can suck honey from the rock and oil of flinty stone ... The secret of his heart is laid open through the clefts of his body; that mighty mystery of loving is laid open. God has even led us by the open clefts into his holy place.[73]

The secret of the heart being laid open through the clefts of the body, and a backwards glance to Bede's image of the pierced heart as the door to Noah's ark, is continued by Bernard's friend and brother Cistercian, William of St Thierry.

> I want to see and touch the whole of him [the crucified Jesus] and … what is more … to approach the most holy wound in his side, the portal of the ark that is there made, and that not only to put my finger or my whole hand into it, but wholly enter into Jesus' very heart, into the holy of holies, the ark of the covenant, the golden urn, the soul of our humanity that holds within itself the manna of the Godhead.[74]

Here, we have not only a visual but also a tactile penetration. Guerric d'Igny, another friend and fellow Cistercian of Bernard, also used Song of Songs 2:14 to encourage the brothers to "build a nest in the rocks" for Christ's wounds and "offer pardon to the guilty and bestow grace on the just".[75]

Aelred of Rievaux (1109–1167) taught that "the blood that flows from the wounds in Christ's side is changed into wine to gladden you (reverse transubstantiation?) …and the water into milk to nourish you".[76]

Caroline Bynum has argued that the change from blood to milk is eased by the fact that "in medieval medical theory breast milk is processed blood" and that "In medieval devotions like the sacred heart, milk and blood are interchangeable, as are Christ's breasts and the wound in his side".[77] Ruth Fulton goes further and makes this even more explicit: "Christ himself is here, in an image well known to all medievalists, envisioned as a mother, the blood flowing from his side transmuted into milk to feed his children, his side wound transmuted into a nipple flowing with the milk of sweetness."[78] Thus, if blood and milk are interchangeable, so are the male and female genders, as another of Bynum's insights seems to make clear.

> Medieval authors do not seem to have drawn as sharp a line as we do between sexual responses and affective responses or between male and female. Throughout the Middle Ages, authors found it far easier than we seem to find it to apply characteristics stereotyped as male or female to the opposite sex. Moreover, they were clearly not embarrassed to speak of all kinds of in language we find physical and sexual and therefore inappropriate to God.[79]

Karma Lochrie, in her *Mystical Acts, Queer Tendencies*, quotes this passage from Bynum and uses it to show how, why, and in what ways medieval concepts of gender and sexuality were extremely ambiguous and, in contemporary language on these matters, "queer". For Lochrie, Christ's bleeding side is at once a lactating breast and a protecting uterus.[80]

Thus, devotion to the wounds of Christ was already a mark of Cistercian spirituality by the middle decades of the twelfth century, but it was not an exclusive mark. It was shared with members of other religious communities and orders, such as the Victorines, the

Benedictines, the Franciscans, and the Dominicans. They placed it at the centre of their increasingly intense liturgies.[81]

Both in *The Mystical Vine* and in his *Tree of Life*, Bonaventure (ca. 1217–1274) proposes a deep and enduring devotion to the crucified Jesus that he believes is appropriate for all Christians, a devotion focused on the sacred heart.[82] His discussion of his proposal moves seamlessly between personal prayer and theology. So it is that after a beautiful passage describing the wound in Christ's heart as a second cause of death after the mortal wound of love, Bonaventure prays:

> Your side was pierced so that the entrance might be opened there for us. Your heart was wounded so that, free from all worldly tribulations, we might live in that Vine, but your heart was so wounded in order that, through the visible wound, we might see the invisible wound of love. For one who ardently loves is wounded by love. How could Christ better show us in his ardour than by permitting not only his body bur his very heart to be pierced by a lance.[83]

The Dominicans Johannes Tauler (d. 1361) and Henrich Suso (ca. 1295–1366), both European contemporaries of Julian and mystics, shared much of their theology with that of Meister Eckhard (ca. 1260–ca. 1328). They were both well-known for their spiritual direction to nuns, which focussed on devotion to the wounds of Christ and the pierced heart. Suso, for example, is said to have been so devoted to the wounded sacred heart that he slashed his own breast and carved the name of Jesus upon it with the blood that flowed.[84] Suso believed that he had experienced a spiritual marriage with Jesus, so he saw himself as a bride, crowned with a garland of fragrant roses, bearing the carved name of Jesus on his chest.[85] Although Suso does not go quite as far as Rupert of Deutz in regarding himself pregnant with Christ, Suso does imagine himself being embraced by Christ as he uncovers his naked soul.[86] In a chapter entitled "A Delightful Colloquy of the Soul with her Spouse Christ, after His Descent from the Cross", in his work *The Soul's Love-Book*, Suso tells his naked soul, "Behold, you have a secure refuge in the deep wound of his heart."[87] I

Suso imagines himself as the submissive female bride, but nevertheless he remains the authoritative male spiritual director. Suso and many male theologians, even to our own time, continue to be responsible for this exegesis, biblical imagery and allegorical treatment in their intense love of the wound in Jesus's side.[88] However, even though men predominate as writers on the spiritual life, and there are poetic mystics amongst them, it is the women (and especially women mystics) who bring an even more intense fervour and passion to the wound in Christ's side and the sacred heart. As Caroline Bynum has argued:

> For the first time in Christian history we can document that a particular kind of religious experience is more common among women than men. For the first time in history certain major devotional and theological emphases emanate from

women and influence the basic development of spirituality.[89]

That devotion and influence is illustrated by the visions at the convent in Helfta, which were granted to Mechtild of Hackeborn (d. 1299) and Gertrude the Great (1256–1302). After this, the development to the sacred heart increases amongst later female mystics.

They were all preceded, of course, by the polymath Hildegard of Bingen (1098–1179), a contemporary of Bernard who acted as her *amicus curae* to Pope Eugenius III. Hildegard found references to the wounds and the pierced heart in the patristics and later writings and adapted them to her medieval audience, especially in her poetry:

> O out poured blood
> that resounded on high
> when all the elements
> folded themselves
> into a voice of lament
> with trembling
> for the blood of their creator
> touched them
> Anoint us!
> Heal our diseases.[90]

We have seen that water and blood flowing from Christ's side was widely recognised as a symbol for the establishment of the Church and her sacraments by Augustine, Bede, and the

Cistercians, amongst others. But in her more artistic and visual representation in Liber Scivas, Hildegaard expands and strengthens the image. She has Ecclesia (the community, the Church) standing in the place and attitude of Mary at the right side of the cross, receiving the blood in a chalice which she (Ecclesia) then offers at the Mass.[91] The motif of a woman (or an angel?) receiving Christ's blood frequently occurs in the iconography of the period,[92] which influenced and was influenced by the devotion to the Sacred Heart.

The mystics of the convent at Helfta, which drew on the Cistercian tradition, such as Mechthild of Magdeburg (ca. 1270–ca. 1282), Mecthild of Hackeborn (1232–1292), and Gertrude the Great (1256–ca. 1302), were instrumental in giving devotion to the Sacred Heart its explicit form and content.[93] In Book 1 of *The Flowing Light of Divinity*, Mechthild of Mageburg describes "The Souls' Trip to Court", in which Christ shows her his divine heart: "it is reddish gold, burning in a large charcoal fire. Then he places her in his ardent heart so that the noble prince and the little servant girl embrace and unite as water and wine".[94] Mechtild also describes a raging fire at the centre of Christ's molten heart and she presents many other vivid images in her account of her visions of the Sacred Heart.

Many of these are drawn from nature, plants, and trees. This is common in medieval mystical writing, such as Gertrude the Great. The soul, for example, is often described as a tree grafted and planted into Christ's side. The tree (her soul) draws a form of sap, which is love, from his heart. This sap of love is the core power of both God and humankind, and it is this that explains how it is that Jesus can be truly a person and truly God.[95] Medieval mystics think of themselves as a plant bowed down and flattened by having been drenched and flooded by divine love, but in this soggy state, she receives a promise of more gentle rains ahead proportionate to her capacity to receive and use them,[96] and this leads to a description of the fluids flowing from Jesus's side, which references John 19:34 and Revelation 22:1. The language is remarkably similar to that of Julian's description of Christ's blood flowing and coagulating, and it is worth quoting here in full to see how this is.

> He extended from his left side, as if from the depths of his Sacred Heart, a liquid stream of purity and the strength of crystal. As it went forth it covered that adorable breast like a collar; it seemed translucent, tinted with gold and rosy pink, flickering between the two colours. While this was happening the Lord added, "The sickness which causes you distress at present has sanctified your soul with the result that whenever, for my sake, you lower yourself to the thoughts, words and deeds, which are not concerned with me, you will never go further from me than is shown you in this stream. Moreover, just as it shines gold and rosy pink through the purity of crystal, as the co-working of my divine nature and the perfect patience of my rosy human nature will be pleasing, suffusing and permeating all that you will."[97]

Gertrude reveals other visions which use similar imagery but are different in content. For example, in another vision she is granted renewed sight of the collar. She delights in seeing it again because it reinforces her sense of being close to Christ, his delight in her as the person she is, and the strength of her faith.[98] On two other occasions, she sees the liquid jet spurting from Christ's side, but in these visions she takes the blood deep into herself through her mouth, drinking it through a straw.[99] It is worth noting that like Julian, Gertrude is full involved in her visions. She sees and hears and is aware of nothing else so that she becomes an active agent in them. Gertrude's visions, especially in book 3, are full of images of spears, bloody wounds, open hearts, and exchanges of love.[100] Like Julian, her visions are not only visual but auditory. For example, Christ's heart is a musical instrument, which accompanies her chant.[101] Like Julian, she too devotes her entire being, body, and soul into her loving and passionate devotion to the Sacred Heart.

Drawing heavily on the Cistercian tradition, both Mecthild and Gertrude apply themselves to the text of the Song of Songs 4:9, "You have wounded my heart, my sister my bride," and see which wounds in Christ's heart are theirs. They regard themselves as having personally thrust the lance into Christ's side.[102] Indeed, they go further; perhaps suggesting that what virtue they have is equally wounding. From a modern point of view, this may seem perverse. We like to think that virtue, or the lack of it, is both innate and acquired. Not so for thirteenth-century nuns for whom there is no such thing as virtue unless it is derived from Christ's loving sacrifice on the cross. Therefore, to suggest that virtue wounds Christ's side is to say that charity and the traditional acts of mercy are the enduring fruits and benefits of Christ's crucifixion.

The nuns of Helfta represent the development of Cistercian theology in relation to pain, suffering, and death, and now we turn to Angela of Foligno (ca. 1248–1309) as one more in the development of feminine thought on the same themes. We should note at the outset her thought owes much to that of Bonaventure, but it is much more passionate and sensuous. Of one vision, she says:

> Then Christ called me and said that I should put my mouth on his wounds in his side. And it seemed to me that I saw and drank his blood flowing freshly from his side. And I was given to understand that by this wound he would cleanse me. And at this I began to feel great joy, although when I thought about the passion I felt sadness. And I prayed to the Lord that he would cause me to shed all my blood for his love, just as he had done for me. And I was so disposed myself on account of his love that I wished all my limbs might suffer a death unlike his passion, that is, a more vile death.[103]

If Angela's language is intense and sensuous, that of another Franciscan, Catherine of Sienna (1347–1380), borders on the erotic. She has a vision which is very similar to Angela's, but it is one in which Christ tenderly draws her to himself as if to kiss her. He provides her with the blood from his side—not, as for Angela, a means of cleansing but as an aphrodisiac milk which echoes and continues the theme of lactation considered earlier.

> With that he tenderly placed his right hand on her neck, and drew her towards the wound in his side "Drink, daughter, from my side", he said, "and by that draught your soul shall be enraptured with such delight that your very body, which for my sake you have denied, will be inundated with its overflowing goodness." Drawn close in this way to the outlet of the Fountain of Life, she fastened her lips upon that sacred wound, and still more eagerly the mouth of her soul, and there she slaked her thirst.[104]

These highly charged and emotional texts find striking counterparts in the art of the period. Some are by and for women. Some of them are simple and "primitive", but all catch our attention and depict a fervid devotion to Christ's wounded side. Flora Lewes has explained:

> Although in the majority of images the five wounds are shown centred on the wounded heart, the earliest images combine the *arma Christi* not with these, but with a single wound: that in Christ's side. Women particularly nuns, played an important part in the creation of these early images ... The wound in Christ's side could be regarded as female and yet

explored by men, as a site of union between sponsus and sponsa, and also of parturition.[105]

The large, red oval shape of the wounds in Christ's side, often depicted as life-sized, frequently resembles female genitals through which the Church is born and into which holy mystery penetrates.[106] The oval image of the wound in Christ's side is transferred to the wound in his heart. As Voaden has remarked concerning the female mystics at Helfta in relation to the Sacred Heart, "The Sacred Heart became a sight of female biological characteristics; it bleeds, it flows, it opens it encloses. Sometimes it is overwhelmingly fleshly. Medieval illustrations of the Sacred Heart resemble nothing so much as a vagina. The wound was graphically represented as a slit between two gaping edges: sometimes, but not always, drops of blood were shown emerging."[107]

Although writers of the patristic and early medieval period associate many flowers, fruits and spices with the Passion,[108] women in the later Middle Ages, largely following the devotional precedent set by Bonaventure,[109] gave the honour to the red rose as the passion flower.[110] Meditation on Jesus covered with blood, as represented by Bernard and by Bonaventure ("Behold how the crimsoned Jesus blossomed forth the rose"), led to some rather disturbing art drawn in convents, such as an image of Bernard and a nun "embracing a cross transformed into a geyser of redeeming blood".[111] Many of these drawings are collected and commented on by Hamburger in *Nuns as Artists: The Visual Culture of a Medieval Convent.*[112]

At the risk of pressing the point, one further example of nuns' art illustrates the extent to which devotion to Christ's wound moved from side to heart in the period before Julian. The disembodied heart became a common image.[113] It was sometimes shown as a chamber in which the devoted "spouse" could embrace her loving Lord as Saviour, often depicted as a child. In Hamburger's description of the St Walburg drawing, *The Heart of the Cross*, "We zoom in on the stunning, even shocking, image of the heart at the centre, penetrating the gash to find ourselves ... in the person of the nun, identified by her habit ... nestled within it, exchanging vows with Christ."[114]

Conclusion

This chapter has shown that in the period before Julian, religious writers, founders of monastic orders, and mystics were enraptured by the Passion of Christ, his wounds, his blood, and especially his Sacred Heart, which expressed in very vivid ways his universal love for everyone. The question remains, however, as to how these understandings may have influenced Julian in the composition of the Showings.[115]

As we know, the first gift that Julian asked for from the Lord was that she see, share in, and experience his Passion and understand the pain of his bodily suffering.[116] She was granted this gift so that she sees his bloody head and face (Showings 1 and 2), and in Showing 4 she sees "the body of Christ bleeding abundantly" so that "the hot blood ran so abundantly that no skin or wound could be seen, it seemed to be all blood". This abundance of blood washes away all trace of human sin, "for there is no liquid created which he likes to give us so much: it is a plentiful as it is precious by virtue of his holy Godhead". Indeed, "the precious plenty of his beloved blood overflows the whole earth and is ready to wash away the sins of all people". In Showing 8, as we will see in another chapter, Julian sees Christ suffering human bodily death, and in Showing 10 Jesus shows Julian his (Sacred?) Heart within his wounded side, saying, "Look how much I loved you."

> Then with a glad face, our Lord looked into his side, and gazed, rejoicing, and with his dear gaze he led his creature's understanding through the same wound into his side. And then he revealed a beautiful and delightful place which was large enough for all mankind who shall be saved to rest there in peace and love. And with this he brought to mind the precious blood and water which he allowed to our out completely for love. And in this dear vision he showed his sacred heart riven in two.[117]

Words and images such as these show the interpretational difference between the early medieval understandings of the pain and wounds of Christ's and those of later mystical visions which this chapter has traced. Texts and iconography from the early medieval period, from Bede onwards, do not hesitate to depict Christ's pain and wounded side, but the later theological exegesis views the Saviour as king and judge, and the Christian as with such embellishments that they are hardly recognisable.

Nevertheless, in the later period we find forms of poetic and graphic language which are more suited to their ardent and passionate devotion. Amongst these, as this chapter has noted, are the tree growing from Christ's wound, the collar, the necklace, his chest, the red rose of his wounds and blood and the water flowing with the transparency of crystal, and the flickering rich colours of his Sacred Heart. Prominent too in the later period is the depiction of Christ's dismembered body: the slash in his heart topped with a crown of thorns or a simple cross, the side wound in female guise as an open vulva accompanied by the instruments of the Passion, nails, whips, scourges, sponges, and weapons of war like the lance.

All these images which this chapter has considered mark the transition in devotion from Christ's wounded side to his Sacred Heart. Together, they culminate in what is surely the final and ultimate *imitatio Christi*—the possibility of "bearing his marks in my body" (Galatians 6:17), the stigmata.

CHAPTER 3

JULIAN OF NORWICH: APOSTLE OF PAIN

Julian's Illness and the Showings

We do not know when Julian wrote her Short Text other than it was very soon after she received the Showings. The Long Text was probably completed in about 1393. The Short Text consists of twenty-five chapters, and the Long Text has eighty-six. In her introduction to the Short Text (Chapters 1–3), Julian explains that she had prayed for three gifts from God. The first was to have "recollection of Christ's Passion", the second was to experience bodily illness, and the third was to receive what she describes as "three wounds".[118] With regard to the first gift, Julian tells us that she already thought that she had an adequate if intellectual understanding of Christ's Passion from the teaching of the Church, but she wanted a more personal and intimate experience, seeing the crucifixion with her own eyes. She wanted to stand by the cross of Jesus alongside Mary and the others and so share his suffering and theirs. She goes on to explain.

> I desired a bodily sight, through which I might have more knowledge of our Lord and saviour's bodily pains, and of the compassion of Our Lady and of all his true lovers who were living at the time and saw his pains, for I would have been one of them and have suffered with them.[119]

Concerning her illness, Julian prayed for the "gift" of bodily illness so severe that she would have what we might nowadays call a near-death experience.

> And in this sickness I wanted to have every kind of pain, bodily and spiritual, which I should have if I were dying ... and every other kind of pain except the departure of the spirit, for I hoped that this would be profitable to me when I should die.[120]

Julian's prayers are answered, and on the fourth night of her illness,[121] she is given extreme unction (the last rights) because it is scarcely possible that she will live to see the new dawn. She survives for another three days, by which time she is so extremely ill that "her curate" is sent for again. Upon his arrival, she is paralysed and has no feeling in her body. She writes that the curate (priest) held a crucifix for her to look at it and to take comfort in it, and perhaps to distract the evident distress. Then, at a time when she truly believes that she will die, all her pain is assuaged and disappears, and she receives the sixteen Showings.

It is in the Showings that she receives the recollection of Christ's Passion and her third desire, "the three wounds": "the wound of contrition, the wound of compassion and the wound of longing with my will for God".[122] These wounds lead her to a mystical union with Jesus, and she considers the illness and the overwhelming pain as divine blessings and the vehicle through which she received the Showings and ultimately her final enlightenment, as described in her theological reflections in the Long Text.

All serious Julian scholars agree that the Long Text was written about twenty years later and is almost four times longer than the Short Text. The Short Text was only a kind of notebook, an immediate record of what she had been shown and her point of departure; most of it reappears in the Long Text. Therefore, the Long Text builds upon and elaborates the Short Text already at hand. After twenty years' reflection and meditation on the Showings themselves, Julian could now write about their theological and epistemological importance and meaning. It is here, in the Long Text, that we have her spiritual wisdom and her theology of divine love, and perhaps also her notion of her universal salvation.[123]

Although we know very little about Julian's life before entering her cell,[124] Mari R. Lichmann[125] has noted that "we do know from the Ancrene Riwle, the Rule of Anchoresses and the Anochorites",[126] that meditations on the sufferings and Passion of Christ formed an integral part of the devotions expected of those leading the enclosed life. As the previous chapter argued, such devotions were not an exception, reserved only for the enclosed, but were instead widespread across Europe in the Middle Ages. Therefore, we can easily imagine Julian meditating on the Showings for twenty years in her solitary cell, and through part of this rigorous practice, she developed her teaching and gained new insights into the deeper spiritual meaning of her experiences before she wrote them into the Long Text.

Julian's painful illness is the vehicle through which she experienced her visions, but her short account of it is nevertheless valuable as one of the very few first-person accounts of pain by an English woman in the Middle Ages. According to Esther Cohen, no woman has left such a graphic description of pain and illness, even if we allow for the history of the devotion to the wounds of the Passion in medieval theology. Cohen says that descriptions of pain are largely the preserve of men and that although "there is no lack of self-descriptive women's writings, the voice of the ill woman is silent on the whole".[127] Moreover, although Julian embraces her pain as a divine gift, there is no hint that she deliberately exposed herself to self-inflicted pain (say, through excessive flagellation) or otherwise engaged in so-called ascetic practices, such as holy anorexia, as many of the saints and mystics examined by Caroline Walker Bynum seem to have done.[128]

Whereas Julian describes and elaborates on the pains she shared with Christ in her Showings, the only information she shares with her readers about her illness—which was so severe that the pain of it brought her near death—is that she was paralysed. Her body was "dead from the middle downwards", then the upper part of her body from her breasts up began to die, and "the greatest pain that I felt was my shortness of breath and the ebbing away of my life".[129] Perhaps disappointingly, we can deduce very little as to what sort of illness this might have been, but Julian's point is to direct us through her pain to the Showings, and it is this which places her firmly in the mystical tradition we have examined, howbeit that College and Walsh have argued it is precisely this that makes Julian's writings unique, at least in England.

> Had it not been that she was convinced that she was divinely commanded to write down her record of her visions, she might have been no more today than one among the many thousands of names of those who in medieval England lived as solitaries for the love of God, but of whom nothing else is known.[130]

Julian's Showings involve all the senses. She experiences what she describes as "bodily sights" and "ghostly sights" (mental and spiritual insights). They involve her whole person. Her pain is both physical and spiritual.

The Showings of the Passion in which Julian experiences body pain occur in Showings seven and eight. Of the sixteen Showings, they are both structurally and theologically the midpoint and form the climax of her visions.

Most of Julian's Showings concern God's divine and all-embracing love and provide insights into God's goodness and care for all creation. One remarkable feature in her Showings is her teaching on the Motherhood of God (from chapter 51 in the

Long Text). This has received considerable attention from scholars and others. It is for these reasons that many people rightly think of Julian as the apostle of love, and it is her theology of divine love that has made her so well-known and caused such great devotion to her by so many through the centuries. It is her emphasis on love that finds an even greater resonance today at a time when love seems to be so rare or is reduced to mere sexual activity. As the introduction noted, however, it is only recently, if at all, that her experience of pain and its links with the content of her Showings have started to receive attention. What follows in the remainder of this chapter is intended as a contribution to that new direction in Julian studies.

Showings Seven and Eight: An Analysis[131]

In Showings seven and eight, Julian's bodily experience of pain comes to the fore. She describes the intensity of her physical pain. In Showing seven (chapter 15),[132] Julian first visualises "supreme spiritual delight"[133] even though in her pain, she feels the abandonment of despair so deeply that she "hardly had the patience to go on living".[134] The creative tension between these two apparently contradictory feelings repeatedly alternates throughout this Showing and demonstrates the anguish of her physical pain and her anxiety in what she believes to be her abandonment. For example:

> And then ... I felt the pain, and then afterwards the delight and the joy, now the one and now the other,

again and again, I suppose about twenty times. And in the time of joy I could have said with St Paul: Nothing can separate me from the Love of Christ; and in the pain I could have said with St Peter: Lord save me for I am perishing ... For it is God's will that we do all in our power to preserve our consolation, for bliss lasts for evermore, and pain is passing, and will be reduced to nothing for those who will be saved. Therefore, it is not God's will that when we feel pain we should pursue it in sorrow and mourning for it, but that suddenly we should pass it over, and preserve ourselves in the endless delight which is God.[135]

In Showing eight (chapters 16–20), Julian experiences a revelation of the pain of Christ's Passion. Her Showing, which she refers to as a "bodily sight", is described graphically and in full. She spares nothing for the imagination! College and Walsh have noted in respect to this revelation that Julian "wishes to show how completely her first prayer was answered, to have recollection of the Passion".[136] Julian continues to describe her own pain, which she refers to as being part of a "ghostly sight".

> This revelation of Christ's passion filled me full of pains, for I knew well that he suffered only once, but it was his will to show it to me and fill me with mind of it, as I had asked before. And in all this time that Christ was present to me, I felt no pain

except for Christ's pains; and then it came to me that I had little known what pain it was that I had asked, and like a wretch I regretted it, thinking that if I had known what it had been, I should have been reluctant to ask for it. For it seemed to me that my pains exceeded any mortal death. I thought: Is there any pain in hell like this pain? And in my reason I answered: Hell is a different pain, for in it there is despair.[137] But of all the pains that lead to salvation, this is the greatest, to see the lover suffer. How could any pain be greater than to see him who is all my life, all my bliss and all my joy suffer? Here I felt unshakeably that I loved Christ so much more than myself that there was no pain which could be suffered like the sorrow I felt to see him in pain.[138]

Next, in chapter 18, Julian is shown the Virgin Mary and Christ's followers at the cross as they mourn him. She feels their grief and shares their pain from love of Christ, "for when he was in pain, we were in pain."[139] I think this reflects the second "wound" for which Julian prayed, that of compassion. Julian is shown Our Lady's compassion for Christ and how those others around him who were close to him felt compassion for Christ and for Mary. From identification with Christ's pains in chapter 17, she now relates how she identifies with the Mother of God and his followers in their sorrow and pain. Julian goes on to explain how all of creation is capable of feeling pain suffered because of Christ's Passion and his blood soaking into the very soil of Calvary.

Indeed, "even those who did not recognise him suffered because the comfort of all creation failed them, except for God's powerful, secret preservation of them".[140] This comes about because of the "great unity between Christ and us".[141]

In chapter 19, Julian is minded to look away from the cross because she can bear the sight of it no longer, and she thinks it better to look towards heaven. She thinks better of it, acknowledging that she "would rather have remained in that pain until Judgement Day than have to come to heaven any other way than by him".[142] Here, Julian shares much with those writers we considered in chapter 2 of this book who believed that it is through the suffering of Christ's pain (*imitatio Christi*) that a place in heaven is gained.

The creative tension between pain and joy gives Julian another insight during this Showing. Although she had previously regretted praying for a share in Christ's bodily pain on the cross, she now realises that this regret is "the reluctance and domination of the flesh", of which her soul does not approve and to which God attaches no blame. It is her exterior, her flesh, that feels regret and pain, whereas her interior being, her soul, is exalted and blessed: "it is all peace and love ... and it was in this part of me that I powerfully, wisely and deliberately chose Jesus for my heaven".[143]

In chapter 20, Julian describes in far more detail how it is that Jesus, who is the "highest and most majestic king", had to suffer one of the most painful deaths ever invented in the whole of human history. Julian apprehends that because of his love for humanity, Jesus "willingly chose suffering with a great desire, and suffered it meekly with a great joy".[144] Julian concludes her account of this Showing with the following summary, in which she returns to the three wounds for which she had prayed.

> It is God's will, as I understand it, that we contemplate the Blessed Passion in three ways. First, that we contemplate with contrition, and compassion the cruel pain he suffered: and our Lord revealed that at this time and gave me strength and grace to see it.[145]

The suffering Julian saw and experienced in her own body and soul, and her sharing in the pain of crucifixion as recounted in the seventh and eight Showings, represents her own *imitatio Christi*. Julian had prayed to share the pains of Christ's passion, so she and her fellow mystics, as we have seen, welcome the pain in order not to lose this focus. When we are fully healthy, we tend to forget our bodies, and this way of "forgetting" seems to be decisive for our ability to fully engage with the world and creatures around us. But for an *imitatio Christi*, the opposite is true. If, like Julian, we want to fully take part in Christ's passion, the body must be the vehicle through which Christ's suffering can manifest itself in the most physical of ways including, for some, the reception of the stigmata. Through physical bodily pain, it becomes quite impossible to forget the body and its pain, so it is precisely through pain that identification with Christ's suffering may be experienced most intensely.

Pain enhances the mystical experience. Because one becomes so aware of the body through the experience of pain, pain becomes the most powerful way of experiencing the compassion (suffering with) and identification with Christ.[146] Due to the intensity of her pain—she and her companions truly believed she was at the point of death because of it—it is impossible for Julian to lose focus on Christ's suffering. She feels it. She experiences it. It is inescapable and ultimately ineffable. Julian focuses on the pain in her body and in the body of the crucified Christ too. They share, embrace, and plunge themselves in each other's pain. Compassion indeed! This is as far from the absent body as it is possible to be, because these are intensely present bodies. Yet this being present is also paradoxical, a paradox which I think applies to Julian as other compassionate mystics. That is, when mystics typically have out-of-body experiences, their bodies become more present than ever. Their ekstasis becomes corporeal.

This way of focussing attention on Christ through bodily suffering is surely one reason for embracing the pain. Although the pain is excessive, a pain beyond description,[147] it also feels secure and safe. In Julian's case, it is so "sweet" that she does not want it to go away. To the contrary, she has prayed for it and rejoices that her prayer has been answered. Perhaps she did not quite know the intensity and implications of that answer. Julian writes, "I would rather have remained in that pain until Judgement Day than have come to heaven any other way than by him."[148]

This also represents a paradox to the modern reader and devotee of Julian for whom, as we mentioned before, pain is something to be medicalised and thereby vanquished. I would argue that the joyful experience of pain is so intimately connected to the intense physical manifestation of suffering that it becomes the most powerful identification with Christ's Passion. Indeed, they are so inextricably linked that it is quite impossible to focus on anything else. Because Julian's desire was to identify with Christ in every single way, this experience of pain is a fulfilment of her desire and her prayer and is thus joyful. But there is also far more to it than this; Christ voluntarily suffered pain with joy because of his compassion for human beings, and Julian desires to suffer the greatest pain for the love of Christ with joy. It was in his suffering that Christ's compassion for all things was revealed to the world. His compassion is the ultimate act of love. Julian desired to demonstrate her love for Christ in imitating his Passion. This becomes the ultimate identification with Christ, and through this pain, Julian experienced complete union with him, without loss of identity on either side—the ultimate joy and telos.

The paradox is retained at the very centre of Julian's painful experience. It is both intensely physical and ecstatic at the same time. It is both physical and spiritual, painful and joyful, all at once and all the time. I would argue that it is in this way that there is an equivalence between physical experience and spiritual ("religious") experience, because Julian's physical pain equals Christ's pain, and *imitatio Christi* is the ultimate spiritual experience. In this way too, the most excessive physical experience of pain—Christ's Passion—corresponds to the most intense spiritual experience.

Theologically, this paradox reflects the paradox of Christ as both truly a person and truly God. It is absolutely in line with the Christian concept that Christ's humanity and incarnation has the ability to feel pain, suffer, and die despite his divinity. Bodily pain belongs to the soul. Because the senses flow from and are subject to the soul, all suffering can be traced back to the soul.[149] Following this Christological idea of Jesus as truly a person, truly God, who physically suffered in his human nature, Julian, in her own *imitatio Christi*, experienced pain through her spiritual Showings.

She experienced union with God both physically and spiritually, and we have seen in a previous chapter how, why, and in what ways her doing so stands in a very long and venerable religious tradition. Julian, like those before her, roots and grounds physical suffering firmly in the context of divine love.

CHAPTER 4

EXPLAINING, INTERPRETING, AND UNDERSTANDING JULIAN'S SPIRITUAL TRANSFORMATION THROUGH PAIN

This chapter considers Julian's transformation from physical suffering and pain and her *imitatio Christi* to spiritual joy and her "one-ing" with God. It will do so by returning to the insights of Paul Ricoeur's hermeneutical arc and applying them to that process of transformation on two levels: the level of Julian's lived experience and the text she left behind.

For Julian, the object of interpretation is her own visions and experiences. According to Ricoeur, the three stages we considered in an earlier chapter need to be taken together in order to obtain critical understanding; it does not come easily because it cannot—hence the idea of an arc rather than a straight line from naïve to critical understanding. As we have seen, the deep understanding which marks the other cornerstone of Ricoeur's arch is also referred to as appropriation. This appropriation at the end of the arch entails not only a new and better understanding of the object of interpretation but also a new understanding of oneself.

Julian's understanding of herself is naïve before her illness sets in, and she receives her visions. As she interprets her own experiences, she appropriates the insights she gains from her interpretation process, and by acquiring these insights, she understands herself in new ways. As such, and in a similar manner as the two circles outlined earlier, the reading or interpretation process works on two levels: it involves both interpretation in order to understand "what the text wants",[150] and through this process, the interpreter comes close to a new understanding of the self—that is, a deeper self-perception or understanding of the "other" or new self.

This encounter between the object of interpretation and the self-perceptive interpreter is what Rudolf Bultmann referred to as "the existential encounter".[151]

In my analysis of Julian's visions which follow, I will suggest that a similar, implicit, hermeneutical approach is at play in her understandings of the visions and of herself. I will illustrate this by applying Ricoeur's method on the material under discussion. This will help us see how Julian's understanding developed between the writing of the Short and Long Texts as she pondered the content of her visions. We will see too how the *imitatio christi* is at play too.

The Level of Experience

Julian's Showings can be read in various ways, not least as a spiritual journey from somewhat naïve theological understanding to deep, critical, and personal experience of the totality of God's all-embracing love for all that was made. By applying Ricoeur's hermeneutical arch to such a reading, we could say that the first pillar on which the arch rests is the naïve Julian praying for a severe illness and a share in Christ's suffering by the three gifts of wounds. Among the many stages of her journey to the next pillar of the arch are her illness (pneumonia, scepsis in the blood?)[152] and the various Showings, of which seven and eight mark the cornerstone of the arch before Julian experiences exalted and joyful Showings of heaven and divine love.

Finally, as we will see, Julian comes out of her Showings and recovers from her illness at the other end of the arch as a "new" Julian living always in the presence of God, with a new perception as to who she is and who God is in Christ. She has deeper insights into God, others, and her own being, which in turn give her a profound understating of and com-passion for "all things seen and unseen".[153] This is the renewed self-perception emphasised by Ricoeur's appropriation.

The climax of Julian's Showings is her physical pain through which she can achieve an *imitatio Christi* and ultimately a "one-ing", a complete unity with God. Often, as noted above, a sick or suffering body turns inwards towards itself because the person concerned can think or feel nothing else. Concepts of God and greater devotion to God may be faraway (except perhaps in blame or exclamation) because the pain is so great. For Julian, however, the opposite was true. Her pain turned her not inwards to herself but outwards towards God and a greater knowledge and union with the divine. As we have repeatedly seen in this book so far, it is Julian's physical painful body which is the vehicle of her Showings, and so it is precisely through her bodily pain that she ultimately unites with God in her *imitatio,* at the other end of the arch. It is because of this experience of "one-ing" with the divine through illness and physical suffering that the pain she feels is sweet and joyful.

The body is the ecstatic, prayerful, and mystical medium through which direct experience of pain becomes Julian's way to God. We could say with some certainty that unless Julian's contemplative senses could be felt in her physical suffering, she has no secure basis for knowing Christ at all. It is, after all, through the pains of the Passion for which she had prayed that Julian receives her first wound. Writing on just this point, College and Walsh noted that Julian

> finds herself repenting her one-time aspiration to suffer the same pains as Christ and those who stand by his cross; but she is enabled, through reasoning, by question and answer to understand that this pain of Christ which she is now sharing is the purification which she had asked for; it is truly redemptive, because it proceeds from her love for him.[154]

This quotation points us towards Julian's own hermeneutical processes, at play through her theological reasoning and interpretation, her questions and answers.

A passage from chapter 17 of the Showings is a case in point.

> I thought: is any pain in hell like this pain? And in my reason I was answered: Hell is a different pain, for in it there is despair. But of all the pains that lead to salvation, this is the greatest, to see the lover suffer. How could any pain be greater than to see him who is all my life, all my bliss and all my joy suffer? Here I felt unshakably that I loved Christ so much more than myself, that there was no pan which could be suffered like the sorrow I felt to see him in pain.[155]

In the hermeneutical process, which is Julian's journey towards "one-ing" with God, the object of interpretation is herself and her mystical experience. She interprets her experiences in her mind and soul as they occur to her and draws conclusions present in her own reasoning. Every new insight leads to the next, but not necessarily in a strictly linear way. Her interpretations and insights twist and interweave with each other, and she is not afraid of returning to an experience or insight where more might be extracted from it. It may be for this reason that she spent twenty years or so between the initial notebook of her experiences (the Short Text) and the final version of her experiences in the Long Text. Even then, Julian does not think that the hermeneutical process is complete. The book has begun, but it is not yet completed.

> This book was begun by God's gift and grace, but according to me it is not yet completed. In love let us all join ... in prayer, in union with God working in us, thanking, trusting, rejoicing. This is how our good Lord wants to be prayed to, as far as I can see from his intention, and the sweet words which were spoken so cheerfully: I am the ground of your beseeching.[156]

That which marks the end of Julian's spiritual transformation—at the far end of the hermeneutical arch, as it were—is the transformation of herself as a result of what she has seen and know in the Showings. The illness which took her to the verge of death may be read as the death of Julian's previous self. The climax is her shared suffering with Christ in his death on the cross, and it is this that marks a rebirth of a new transformed self, a self fully "oned" with God and all created things.

Thus, Christ's Passion is her passion to the extent that spiritual death and rebirth (resurrection?) underscores her *imitatio Christi*. For Julian, death and rebirth of the self has taken place in and through her identification with Christ. They mark a transition from a somewhat theologically naïve young woman to a more reflective, more insightful self.[157] Moreover, this transition leads to yet another phase in her spiritual journey and maturity, because Passion generates compassion, one of her desired wounds. Julian's compassion becomes for her, and for her readers ever since, a paradigm example of the gains that may come from pain. They contribute to the perfection of her soul through pain—the appropriation of her desires and insights. It is in this way that the compassion generated from passion highlights the medieval idea that pain, far from being something to be medicalised and vanquished, had a meaning and purpose. Her pain and *imitatio* gave Julian a new paradigm of regeneration and one which is entirely consistent with the medieval theological understandings of pain which I considered in an earlier chapter.

In her interesting but widely overlooked discussion of how the conversion literature of the seventeenth century may be thought of as a forerunner of modern photography, Ann Hawkins writes of a "regeneration paradigm".[158] I contend her term is equally appropriate for the hermeneutical arch outlined with regard to Julian's spiritual transition because the "regeneration paradigm" entails "the belief that it is possible to undergo a process of transformation so profound as to be experienced as a kind of death to the 'old self' and rebirth to a new and very different self".

Julian enters her spiritual transformation eagerly and voluntarily, with a desire to undertake participation in Christ's passion in recognition of Christ's volitional suffering for all created things. It is that intentionality of Julian's experience and desire to suffer which leads to her unification of her body and soul with the heart of God. Her suffering was willed, desired, and chosen and so becomes part of a much larger context, meaning, and purpose. Her suffering and her self is transformed into something far more than they were before the Showings began. Her interpretation of herself goes through God in her imitation of Christ, as one stage in process of transformation. In becoming one with Christ through imitation and identification, Julian's knowledge of herself and God converge. It is through this appropriation of her experiences that Julian finally acquires knowledge of God. Julian comes to the other end of Ricoeur's arc as a new self, a different "other" than the Julian who entered the hermeneutical process.

As Julian reaches the end of her journey of spiritual transformation as a new self, her last vision fades. Her illness departs, and the spiritual storm she experienced blows away, leaving her with an influx of new insights into what the visions meant and culminated in the conclusion that love was Christ's meaning. As Christ suffered for and with all things, so Julian suffered her pain through her love of Christ. Her pains were granted her as an answer to prayer through God's love for her and a means through which her soul could be perfected and where she would now find the joy of knowing and long God in his fullness.

This is, of course, prefigured in the ninth Showing, which comes immediately after her painful experiences have begun to subside. It is here that we first see her shift from one of pain to complete joy. In the ninth Showing, we begin to glimpse not only the inextricable connection between Christ's solidarity with us in his human nature but also the equally intimate connection between human joy and the glory of God in heaven. Whatever the source of human joy, it is always a foretaste of heavenly joy and final union with God.

Joy and final union with God are the telos of all her Showings, but it can only be attained through *imitatio Christi*. Thus, the painful experience of identification with Christ points directly to the ultimate meaning, which is the highest joy and bliss. Julian recovers from her near-death experiences, but she does so as a fundamentally different person. She is spiritually transformed from the "other" Julian who commenced her spiritual journey by praying for illness and suffering. Now she sees herself in a new way, and it is this transformed self-awareness that leads to union with God. For Julian, it is quite impossible to know God and be united with him without first undergoing the transformative process of *imitatio Christi*.

In this hermeneutic dynamic between the interpreter who continuously adjusts her preconceptions and her naivete in the inner dialogue with herself as she experiences her Showings, their meanings are revealed to Julian in accordance with Colossians 3:10, and she puts on "the new self, which is being renewed in knowledge of its Creator."

The Textual Level

In this section, I argue that Julian's spiritual transformation is reflected and indeed embedded in the text of the Showings. The development of her writing during the twenty years or so from the Short Text to the Long Text marks this hermeneutical process. On the textual level, the first cornerstone of Ricoeur's arc is her naïve interpretation in the short text. Here, Julian has written down her experiences more or less as they appeared to her. The Short Text is an immediate record, a notebook. She has not yet had time to reflect on them or digest her experiences in ways which later allow her to extract their full theological meaning and significance. That is precisely what the twenty years between the two texts are all about. They are years in which she ruminates and contemplates the Showings, and they give her the opportunity to put into words not just her experiences but the enduring wisdom gained from her visions. They are years in which she can practice and test their practical implications and utility as spiritual director and advisor to those from far and near who visited the street window of her solitary cell.

It is for these practical reasons that the Long Text is far more theologically sophisticated than the Short Text, and it accounts for the revisions, additions, and omissions on which scholars have spent much time and energy. Some insights did not work in building up the faith of other "even-christiens". I am not alone in thinking that Julian used the twenty years between texts to test the theological practicality of her visions, and College and Walsh have this to say about the revision in the eighth Showing in which Julian describes her painful turmoil:

> the long text here may seem to lose some of its clarity and force which the short text has when it cites from the Christological hymn in Chapter 2 of Philippians .... *She may have decided that Paul's words were not so apposite as she had once thought.* He is inviting the Philippians to imitate Christ's humility and obedience, *not* to directly experience his bodily sufferings. Doubtless she also found it inappropriate to exhort others to share in his

experience, as she had done, especially since she discovers that she herself can hardly tolerate her participation in his pains.[159]

I suggest that Julian's reliance on St Paul, and then its absence, does not leave a scriptural void. Rather, during the twenty years of rumination, Julian moves from Pauline to Johannine theology. Is there not a parallel between Julian's physical experiences and the Word becoming flesh? As the Word became flesh in the incarnation, in a similar manner, Julian's theology is incarnated in the physicality of her sickness and Showings. It is as though the Word becomes flesh in her flesh. Once united with her, the Word renews itself as Word, being theologically expressed in her theology of the body in the Long Text. If I am right about this, then it would seem to follow that Julian's written text becomes a hermeneutic of the text which is now written into her body and her Showings.

It is in this way, then, that the various stages of Ricoeur's arc are marked by Julian's contemplation and interpretation of various aspects of her Showings, of each new insight she gains during her twenty years of contemplation and development in her theology. What she has seen, and the various levels and layers of meaning, continue to perplex her for these twenty years, but she also continuously arrives at new and deeper insights, which themselves mark new stages of the hermeneutical arch of interpretation. Christ's body and passion are always at the centre of her devotion and her writing.

In fact, the Long Text marks the cornerstone at the other end of the arch. With the composition of the Long Text, Julian has arrived at a deep understanding of her Showings, their theological meaning, and their significance in the community of faith. That does not imply that the work of contemplation on the Showings has ended. Julian says that it must not, because it cannot.

> This book was begun by God's gift and grace, but according to me it is not yet completed. In love let us all join ... together in prayer, in union with God working in us, thanking, trusting, rejoicing. This is how our good Lord wants to be prayed to, as far as I can see from his intention, and from the sweet words which were spoken so cheerfully: "I am the ground of your beseeching.[160]

Nevertheless, Julian has arrived at a new and critical understanding of what her showings were all about: an understanding revealed in her more fully developed theology of love which is *The Showings of Divine Love*.

CHAPTER 5

CLOSING THOUGHTS

Julian's long version of her Showings from circa 1393 is the final testimony of her spiritual journey. Her journey began more than twenty years earlier when she, as a naïve woman, prayed to God to receive severe illness, to experience and imitate Christ's Passion, to receive the three wounds of contrition, and to receive compassion for her fellow Christians and a longing for God. Julian's prayers were heard; she received her visions while lying in such pain that it brought her close to death. The intensity of this pain is recounted in Showings seven and eight, and even now we might find it painful to read.

It is not without significance that all Julian's desires are related to and described in terms of pain. As I have tried to demonstrate in this book, pain was a central theme in medieval theological thought, and the foremost idea was to imitate Christ's passion and identify with his suffering (*imitatio Christi*). The goal of the *imitatio Christi* was and is a harmony with God.

In writing this book, I wanted to explore three questions, the first being in what way the experience of physical pain is both significant and necessary for Julian's *imitatio Chrisiti* and her ultimate goal of union (one-ing) with God. I showed that this was an important theological topic during the medieval period, revolving around a renewed and expanded interest in Christ's human nature and whether and to what extent Christ has been able to experience physical suffering during his Passion. I explained too how, in the later Middle Ages, the idea was nevertheless that the incarnated Christ was fully human (and fully divine) and that he therefore suffered physically just like any other human being. In fact, he suffered voluntarily for the love of all humankind and all creation. This view was the point of departure for Christian devotion, especially amongst those who, like Julian, desired to take a share in his pain. Like Christ, they suffered voluntarily, they prayed to experience pain, and they did so through their love of Jesus. Just as they believed Christ had rejoiced in his suffering for humanity, so they rejoiced in their pain with and for Christ. Therefore, because of the belief that Christ had truly suffered physically, Julian's pain had to be real and physical if she were to properly and devoutly imitate him.

Indeed, from a phenomenological perspective, I have argued that when we are in pain, we become focussed on our bodies and our pain. The body's presence becomes inescapable when it suffers physically, whereas when it functions as we believe it should, without pain, we are only scarcely aware of our bodies. It is, according to Leder, "absent". When Julian suffers physically in her imitation of Christ, she becomes fully focussed on her body and pain, which is also Christ's pain. As such, it is through the body that she can focus most intensely on Christ and subsequently experience union with him.

My second question was to see how her painful experiences contributed to Julian's spiritual journey and development. The question is hopefully answered previously in my book. Moreover, through her pain, she first receives the wound of contrition because she experiences regret for ever having desired such excessive pain. She thinks that her pain, far from being a sharing of Christ's passion, must be demonic. But then she realises that this pain is very different indeed from the pains of hell. The pain of hell is full of despair, whereas her pain (and Christ's) are sweet and joyful, full of love and compassion; it is salvific. Through this joyful pain, she develops her second wound of compassion. She shares in the pain of the Virgin Mary and the disciple whom Jesus loved at the crucifixion. These two wounds are prerequisites for the third wound which is her own longing for an ever-deepening knowledge of God. This she receives at the end of her spiritual journey.

In my analysis, I have shown the details and stages of this spiritual transformation by applying Ricoeur's hermeneutical arc (considered in some detail in chapter 1), which spans from naïve understanding to appropriation. Julian's painful experience of the Passion comes to a developmental climax in her *imitatio Christi*. She experiences the death of her old, naïve self and a rebirth to a new, enlightened, and godlier self. At the end of Julian's journey, she comes to know both herself and God in new ways. She has, in Ricoeurian terms, appropriated her hopes, dreams, visions, and insights.

Despite all this, Julian does not manage to express them systematically for over twenty years. In her first attempt to do so, immediately after the initial showings in the Short Text, the insights she received are not properly digested, and their implications both for the prayer and ethics of her fellow Christians are not thought through. This being the case, she embarks on a new spiritual journey until she arrives at the Long Text.[161]

My third and final question asked whether the tension between the physical and spiritual on the one hand and the unpleasant yet sweet pain on the other may be explained phenomenologically. I have demonstrated that these two paradoxes are closely related. The mystical painful experience involves a bodily presence, but it also involves a loss of self, an out-of-body, near-death experience. Christ suffered with joy for his love of humanity and creation, and so too does Julian find joy that leads to a loss of self.

Julian's whole mystical experience thus becomes a phenomenological paradox. The body is ever present in its painful negativity, but it is also joyous precisely because of this loss of self. It is in this act of love that Julian, in her *imitatio Christi*, loses her old self and is transformed into a new and more insightful self in which she has appropriated all he experiences. Thus, because her experiences are inseparable from pain, Julian becomes for us not just the apostle of God's love for which she is well-known but the Apostle of Pain.

APPENDIX

JULIAN OF NORWICH AND COVID-19, CORONAVIRUS: A PASTORAL RESPONSE

Here, I examine some parts of *The Showings of Divine Love* and consider how Julian of Norwich might inspire us in a sensitive, pastoral approach to those diagnosed with COVID-19 in the UK, and especially those for whom we are immediately responsible both in our churches and in the wider community

In one of his daily press conferences, Prime Minister Boris Johnson told the nation that the present pandemic of COVID-19 is perhaps the most severe health crisis that our nation has had to face and manage in peacetime.[1] The same could easily have been said in fourteenth-century England, a time of bubonic plague, floods, food shortages and famine, widespread social collapse and injustice, and the Hundred Years' War. The plague killed rich and poor alike in vast numbers. At least one-third of the population of Norwich, then England's second city, was killed by recurring outbreaks of the disease from 1348 well into the following century. Widespread fear and panic swept the nation in the face of the disease, and acute personal and communal suffering were dominant aspects of Julian's time. It is against and within this context, and perhaps as a direct response to the suffering and anxiety of her "even christiens" about her, that Julian writes so wonderfully about God's compassion and the love of the divine feminine for all people in *The Showings of Divine Love*.[2]

As someone deeply acquainted with Julian's writing, I can easily see parallels between Julian's time and our own as we learn to cope with COVID-19 amongst us. No doubt new treatments will eventually be found, but until then, the present pandemic remains the primary issue in the UK today. This harsh reality continues to be the pressing pastoral concern for all Christians throughout the world. We can do little about that, but we do have specific and urgent responsibility to find a systematic theological response for those in our care in all our churches across Stroud. The case for this is even more urgent in the light of the closure of churches for all but the occasional private prayer. Here, I want to consider how Julian's theology may be relevant to us in this situation.

COVID-19 will not soon go away. Diagnosis comes as a shock to the individual. The subjective experience remains one of personal disaster. As with any life-threatening condition, the person is affected by the practical implications and limitations, as well as the many complex existential questions that inevitably arise. For those people with a religious background, these challenging questions of meaning are explored, understood, and misunderstood in the context of their religious experience, past and present.

Stigma and the Apportionment of Blame

As times goes by, additional challenges may occur if stigma and an apportionment of blame attaches to a diagnosis of COVID-19 in ways which are not associated with other infections, with the possible exception of HIV/Aids. The sociologist Erving Goffman described stigma as having the effect of reducing a person from being "whole and usual" to "tainted" and to be "discounted" in eyes of others in ways which are "deeply discrediting" to both parties.[3] It will be extremely hard for anyone diagnosed with COVID-19 to escape the impact of stigma as both internally and externally encountered experience.

Those of us engaged in Christian pastoral ministry at whatever level surely already recognise that the stigmatisation of people can often be the most powerful obstacle to effective prevention, treatment, and care.

Taking stigma seriously from our pastoral perspective, we must acknowledge the ways in which the religious experience we have encouraged in those in our congregations and elsewhere may have contributed to this stigma and may continue to do so unless we are very careful indeed. How have we contributed to the alienating discrimination and the internalised guilt and shame that may be a burden to those diagnosed with COVID-19, and certainly those who self-identify as Christians?

One of the major problems is the long and wholly unnecessary association in the church between disease and sin. Too often, even now, and despite Jesus's condemnation of such association during his healing of the man born blind as recounted at John 9, we still read suffering as God's retributive punishment for sin and the ingrained dualism which has informed so much of Western theology seeing "the flesh" as somehow demonic, unholy, and inherently sinful. This forms an extremely unhealthy and unfortunate inheritance that affects our behaviour and the behaviour of those to whom we are called to serve. I have no doubt that some people will feel compelled (or be forced by ministers steeped in this inheritance) to consider whether their infection with COVID-19 is a type of punishment or a consequence of personal "sin".

I have already heard it said that COVID-19 is God's punishment for the "wickedness" of our liberal democracy and especially our recent quest for justice, equality, inclusion, and acceptance of sexual and gender difference beyond the historic division of male and female. This wholly ignores what St Paul has to say on the point of all differences in the Christian community of faith.[4]

It has also been said that COVID-19 is God's way of bypassing human free will and agency and cleaning the world, which is necessary because of our neglect of climate change. It will apparently be accompanied by a new spiritual reformation and revival.

Well, perhaps. But such things are not conducive to effective and loving pastoral care because they are idle speculation, unverifiable, and theologically improbable. Rather, for those coming to us for pastoral care, these are amongst the first challenges we need to address. A person's identity and self-understanding, as well as one's relationship and perception of God, are already called into question in the most dramatic way without our adding to it.

Affectively, stigma and the apportionment of blame is a kind of spiritual violence, an assault on the dignity of a person. Effectively, they exclude a person from full participation in the Christian community and damage the person spiritually insofar as the degree to which it threatens to extinguish a person's sense of the reality of God's unconditional love for the person. When this happens, the person may succumb to and be hindered by that ignorance of which Julian wrote:

> God wants us to consider and enjoy love in everything. And this is the knowledge of which we are most ignorant; for some of us believe that God is almighty and has power to do everything, and that he is all wisdom and knows how to do everything, but that he is love and is willing to do everything—there we stop. And it seems to me that this ignorance is what most hinders those who love God.[5]

Stigma and the apportionment of blame damages a person's own loveliness before God and one's faith in God—who is love by way of identity and not mere predication. Julian is unequivocal and calls this tendency a huge obstacle in the way of a person making spiritual progress, deepening and widening the relationship with God. She goes on to suggest that such a sinful focus (for that is what it is) is "foul ignorance and wickedness".[6]

Julian's Pastoral Advice

Julian's awareness of the long-held ecclesial emphasis on sin, judgement, and suffering in the matter of disease reflects a personal reality which may be encountered in our ministry with people diagnosed with COVID-19 and other illnesses. In case I have not been clear, the present pandemic may expose our preoccupation with sin: Cleanliness is next to godliness). You have the virus, so you are not clean. It follows therefore that you are not, and cannot be, close (next) to God. This, in turn, may surface as a type of problematic spiritual symptom of COVID-19 for the individual. Therefore, I think it important to re-emphasise that for infected people, this burdensome sense of culpability is entirely inappropriate, and those of us in ministry must avoid it altogether. In short, and perhaps not surprisingly, I agree with Julian and understand this preoccupation as the greatest hindrance to spiritual health and well-being, and indeed all forms of faithful discipleship.

Julian says that sin can only be recognised by its effects, by the sufferings it causes. Sin has no existential reality, because sin is non-being. She considers at great length how it is at all possible that the effects of sin can and do exist alongside an all-loving, all-purposeful God, a God who is present in "all things seen and unseen"[7] and in all events. Theologically, we call this the "theodisic problem" which, despite many attempts to do so, has remained largely unresolved throughout Jewish and Christian history. That it has not been resolved forms another obstacle in the minds of many, and that obstacle is so large that it prevents them from joining or having any meaningful contact with communities of faith.

In the thirteenth Showing, Jesus repeatedly reassures Julian that despite sin and suffering, "all shall be well, and all shall be well, and all manner of things will be well".[8] Usually and shamefully omitted from this well-known yet most misquoted and most abused saying of Julian are the words that Jesus speaks by way of preface: "Sin is behovenly" (befitting/necessary).[9] Julian's pondering upon this entire sentence can be considered to be the central and primary theme of all her encounters with Jesus and the entire text which followed the fruit of her meditation on the theodisic problem.

Wisely, Julian does not attempt to resolve the theodisic problem. But she does address our own individual tendencies to judge, apportion blame, and make hard and fast rulings about people and events, which she understands as a human limitation. In the light of modern psychology, Fr Robert Llewelyn (former guardian of Julian's anchorhold in Norwich) interprets this a "human projection" of juridical attributes to God.[10] My late friend and former academic colleague Grace Jantzen viewed the apportionment of blame in the matter of suffering as a function of the Church reminding us of the severity of sin and our need for personal and collective healing in our fractured and broken lives.[11]

Both views may have merit according to our theological stance and outlook, but Julian's overwhelming concern is pastoral. It is as though she puts sin in the context and place to which it properly belongs. We can see this when she insists that *"I saw no substance in sin"*.[12] Like St Augustine of Hippo before her, she wholly and entirely rejected the pernicious dualistic heresy which proposes that evil exists in its own right and that the human body, the world, and all created things are evil. Such dualism (including notions of an eternal war between God and some kind of devil, which has already been won by God, but the devil persists in ongoing skirmishes) is Manachaeism. It is not biblical. It is neither Christian nor particularly well thought through—that is precisely why it is heresy. Rather, for Julian, our bodies, including our sexuality and gender and all created matter, matter because they affirm the omnipotence and immanence of God. Accordingly, they are blessed, having an inherent goodness about them because they come from and return to God: "everything that is done is done well because our Lord does everything … for he is (at) the centre of everything".[13] In this way, Julian affirms her belief in the ultimate goodness of God's creation despite (or because of) the limits of our human imagination and fears.

Nevertheless, Julian challenged the prevailing medieval understanding when she pondered the meaning of "sin is behovenly, but all shall be well". Whereas part of St Augustine's answer to the theodisic problem was concerned with the fact that human beings will always want to deny their culpability for sin and impugn God's righteous anger and punishment, Julian worried that her "even Christiens" will be simply overwhelmed by their guilt for sin and their fear of an angry and vengeful God. That is, whereas Augustine focussed on the causes of sin, Julian is concerned with its consequences.

Julian argues that sin, disease, and suffering are necessary because they serve the beneficial functions of achieving self-knowledge and knowledge of God. Disease in particular provides us with multiple opportunities to understand our own weakness and run towards God's all-encompassing, loving embrace.[14] Sin is therefore pedagogical: it teaches us about ourselves and ourselves in relation to God's loving presence with us every moment of every day.

Julian concentrates far less on the supposed "original sin" of Adam, or personal guilt, preferring instead the Passion of Christ as the ultimate act of love. It is through the Passion alone that sin is behovenly and that all manner of things shall be well, including pandemics (for her, the Black Death; for us, COVID-19). Again, Julian insisted that in these circumstances, the power of God's grace will turn "bitterness into hopes of mercy" and "shame into glory and greater joy; for our generous Lord does not want his servants to despair ... our falling cannot prevent him from loving us".[15]

This is surely the narrative we need to proclaim in all our churches and local communities as we minister in these strange times.

Her emphasis remains on God's total love, compassion, and understanding of us in our affliction, however acquired or encountered. Julian wrote of a God who neither blames us nor considers us guilty:

It is true that sin *may* be a cause of suffering; but all shall be well and all shall be well, and all manner of things shall be well These words were said very tenderly, with no suggestion that I nor anyone else who will be saved was being blamed.[16]

Towards Our Pastoral Response

This national crisis provides a golden opportunity to reflect carefully upon our own thoughts and responses to COVID-19. Each of us must be challenged to reconsider our deeply held attitudes towards sin, disease, stigma, and blame, even and especially where their negative effects are unintended. This is the time to reconsider our fundamental understandings of who we are, who God is, and what we are really called to do with him and in his name. For all our Christian communities of whatsoever denomination, COVID-19 may provide an opportunity to revisit our ministerial, missional, and pastoral theology and practice. As we do so, we might heed Julian's warnings against the false thinking which comes to us when faced with a task of this magnitude, of falling into despair that we simply cannot cope and thereby forgetting the holy and blessed consideration of our everlasting friend.[17]

We must be reminded of and live in hope, that blessed and basic tenet of our faith that Julian was so inspired to express. God is a God of love. He loves us so much that he is head over heels and crazy about us, so much that he wanted to be part of us, one of us, simply because he loves. This is a God who is faithful to us "in weal and in woe"[18] and "constantly in love-longing towards us while we live",[19] as Julian put it. God is a perfect mother who loves us no matter what, and we should run to her skirts to ask for help, or to be lifted up once more to be kissed and embraced.[20] This is a God from whom, despite anything and everything, we can never be parted.[21]

Appendix Notes

1 This is a convenient political forgetting. It wholly overlooks the HIV/AIDS crisis of the 1980s and the fear, isolation, stigma, and blame that was present at the time.

2 Julian of Norwich, *Showing of Divine Love*. Many versions, so-called translations, and paraphrases are available. Amongst the most popular and certainly accessible is *Revelations of Divine Love*, translated by Grace Warrack and modernised by Yolande Clark, with an introduction by A. N. Wilson (London: SPCK, 2017). The quotations of Julian's writing here are from *Showing of Love*, translated by Julia Bolton Holloway (Collegeville, MN: Liturgical Press, 2003).

3 E. Goffman, *Stigma: Notes on the Management of Spoiled Identity* (New York: Simon & Schuster, 1986), 2–5.
Goffman wrote in a pre-HIV/AIDS, pre-COVID-19 time. He wrote of the stigma and blame which attaches to those detained in mental asylum hospitals, but by changing the circumstances (*mutatis mutandis*), his words may still be usefully employed here.

4 Galatians 3:28.

5 Julian Long Text (LT) 73.

6 Julian LT 73.

7 The Nicean-Chalcedonian Creed.

8 Julian LT 23.

9 Julian LT 23.

10 Fr Robert Llewelyn, *With Pity, Not with Blame: The Spirituality of Julian of Norwich and the Cloud of Unknowing for Today* (London: Darton, Longman and Todd, 2003), 20–23.
11 Grace Jantzen, *Julian of Norwich*, (London: SPCK, 2000), 199–200.
12 Julian LT 27.
13 Julian LT 11.
14 Luke 15:11–24.
15 Julian LT Julian LT 27; my emphasis added.
16 See especially Julian LT 76.
17 Julian LT 52.
18 Julian LT 71.
19 See especially Julian LT 61.
20 Romans 8:38; Julian LT 72.
21 Julian LT 24. On the sort of freedom I am referencing here, see Galatians 5:13.

ENDNOTES

1. G. Kneller, *Movements in Thought in Modern Education* (New York: Macmillan, 1984), 103–107.
2. Paul Ricoeur, *Interpretation Theory: Discourse and the Surplus of Meaning* (Fort Worth, TX: Christian University Press, 1976), 95–110.
3. For more on this see, De Censo, *Hermeneutics and the Disclosure of Truth: A Study in the Work of Heidegger, Gadamer and Ricoeur* (Charlottesville, VA: North Western University Press, 1990).
4. Paul Ricoeur, "The Hermeneutical Function of Distanciation", translated by D. Pellauer *Philosophy Today* 17, no. 2–4: 129141.
5. Paul Ricoeur, "Metaphor and the Main Problem of Hermeneutics", *New Literary History* 6, no. 1 (1974): 65–110.
6. Paul Ricoeur, *Hermeneutics and the Human Sciences*, edited by J. B. Thompson(CUP, 1981), 112–119.
7. Paul Ricoeur, "The Hermeneutical Function of Distanciation", 129–141.
8. M Allen and I Jensen: Hermeneutical Inquiry: Meaning and Scope. Western J Nursing Res, 12 (2) pp241-253.
9. For more on this point and the importance of not confusing distanciation with objective knowledge, see M. Heidegger, *Being and Time* (Oxford: Basil Blackwell, 1962).
10. Gunter Grass, *The Tin Drum*, English translation (New York: Pantheon Books, 1962).

11 See Ricoeur, "The Hermeneutical Function of Distanciation".
12 Ricoeur, *Hermeneutics and the Human Sciences*, 112–128.
13 Ibid.
14 See Ricoeur, "The Hermeneutical Function of Distanciation".
15 Ricoeur, "The Hermeneutical Function of Distanciation".
16 Ricoeur, *Interpretation Theory*, 95–110.
17 Ricoeur, *Hermeneutics and the Human Sciences*, 112–128.
18 Ricoeur, "The Hermeneutical Function of Distanciation", 129–141.
19 Ricoeur, "Metaphor and the Main Problem of Hermeneutics", 65–110.
20 Ricoeur, *Hemeneutics and the Human Sciences*, 112–128.
21 Ricouer, *Hermeneutics and the Human Sciences*, 112–128.
22 Ricoeur, *Hermeneutics and the Human Sciences*, 112–128
23 Ricoeur, "Metaphor and the Main Problem of Hermeneutics", 65–110; Ricoeur, *Hermeneutics and the Human Sciences*, 112–128.
24 Hans-Georg Gadamer, "The Universality of the Hermeneutical Problem", translated by D. Lange, in *The Hermeneutic Tradition from Ast to Ricoeur*, edited by G. Ormiston and A. Scrift (New York: Albany State University Press, 1990), 147–158.
25 J. Higgins, "Raymond Williams and the Problem of Ideology", in *Postmodernism and Politics*, edited by J. Arac (Minneapolis: University of Minneapolis Press, 1986), 112–122.
26 Ricoeur, "Metaphor and the Main Problem of Hermeneutics"; Ricoeur, *Hermeneutics and the Human Sciences*.
27 J. Higgins, "Raymond Williams and the Problem of Ideology", 112–122.
28 Ricoeur, "The Hermeneutical Function of Distanciation", 129–141; Ricoeur, "Metaphor and the Main Problem of Hermeneutics", 65–110.
29 F. Jameson, *The Ideology of Theory: Essays 1971–1986*, vol. 1 (Minneapolis: University of Minneapolis Press, 1986), 69.
30 Ricoeur, *Lectures on Ideology and Utopia*, edited by G. Taylor (New York: Columbia University Press, 1986), 56–93.
31 Ricoeur, *Hermeneutics and the Human Sciences*, 112–128.
32 Ricoeur, *Hermeneutics and the Human Sciences*, 112–128.
33 Paul Ricoeur, *Time and Narrative*, vol. 1 (Chicago: University of Chicago Press, 1984).
34 This shift in devotional sensibility has been variously remarked upon by many historians and theologians. For a recent synthesis of their thinking, see Rachel

Fulton, *From Judgement to Passion: Devotion to Christ and the Virgin Mary 800–1200* (New York: Columbia University Press, 2002).

35 S. Kemp, *Medieval Psychology* (New York: Greenwood Press, 1990).
36 Philip Ziegler, *The Black Death* (London: Collins, 1969).
37 Jack Hartnell, *Medieval Bodies—Life, Death and Art in the Middle Ages* (London: Profile Books, 2018).
38 Laura A. Fink, "Mystical Bodies and the Dialogics of Vision", in *Maps of Flesh and Light—The Religious Experience of Medieval Women Mystics*, edited by Ulrike Wiethaus (New York: Syracuse University Press, 1993); Ellen Ros, "She Wept and Cried Right Loud for Sorrow and Pain—Suffering, the Spiritual Journey, and Women's Experience in Late Medieval Mysticism", in *Maps of Flesh and Light—The Religious Experience of Medieval Women Mystics*, edited by Ulrike Wiethaus (New York: Syracuse University Press, 1993).
39 Ester Cohen, *The Modulated Scream: Pain in Late Medieval Culture* (Chicago: University of Chicago Press, 2009).
40 This seems to be a somewhat extreme position to take. It is not at all clear what "pain itself" might be because it cannot be known or observed apart from a body (or mind) which suffers it. Therefore, I would modify Cohen's statement by arguing that we all know pain even if, in the end, we know only our own pain. Other people's pain cannot be known, but it can be observed, and precisely through that observation, we can find empathy with the sufferer from the foundation of our own experiences.
41 Cohen, *The Modulated Scream*. Medieval perceptions and attitudes to pain will be considered below in a later chapter.
42 Cohen, "The Expression of Pain in the Later Middle Ages: Deliverance, Acceptance and Infamy", in *Bodily Extremities: Preoccupations with the Human Body in Early Modern European Culture*, edited by F. Egmond and R. Zwijnenberg (Farnham: Ashgate, 2003), 195–219.
43 Cohen, "The Expression of Pain in the Later Middle Ages", 195–196.
44 John 9:1–12.
45 Drew Leder, *The Absent Body* (Chicago: University of Chicago Press 1990).
46 Leder, *The Absent Body*, 69.
47 Leder, *The Absent Body*, 11–35.
48 Leder, *The Absent Body*, 69–100.
49 Leder, *The Absent Body*, 73.
50 Leder, *The Absent Body*, 73.

51 Leder, *The Absent Body*, 74.
52 Philippians 2:8.
53 My emphasis added.
54 See especially Gerhard Kittle, ed., *The Theological Dictionary of the New Testament* (Grand Rapids, MI: Erdmans, 1965).
55 The name Longinous is derived from the instrument the soldier used (Greek lOch, "lance").
56 Pierre Barbet, *A Doctor at Calvary—The Passion of Our Lord Jesus Christ as Described by a Surgeon* (New York: P. J. Kennedy, 1953). See chapter 7, "The Wound of the Heart". It is unfortunate that he uses "side" as a synonym for "right".
57 According to the Anchor Bible, "the Ethiopic specifies that it was the right side, a specification that also appears in the apocryphal works Acts of Pilate and has guided artistic reproductions of the scene" (935).
58 Ezekiel 47:2.
59 These verses have caused enormous controversy amongst exegetes and are well summarised in the Anchor Bible (320–323).
60 My emphasis added.
61 See Aelred of Rievaux, *The Mirror of Charity*, translated by Elizabeth Connor (Kalamazoo, MI: Cistercian Publications, 1990); Aelred of Rievaux, *On Love and Order in the World and the Church*, translated by John R. Sommerfelt (New York: Newman Press, 2006). See also Bernard of Clairvaux, *On the Spirituality of Relationship*, translated by John R. Sommerfelt (New York: Newman Press, 2004).
62 See Augustine Sermon 5 (PL38.55).
63 Bede, *Homilies on the Gospels*. Homily II.4, translated by Lawrence T. Martin and Davis Hurst (Kalamazoo, MI: Cistercian Publications, 1991).
64 Bede, *In Epistulas Septem Cathoicas*. I 1 lon. V 7–8, CCSL 121, p. 321.
65 Bede, Homily II.9, 82–83; CCSL 122, Homilia II, 9 p. 242.
66 Bede, *A Biblical Miscellany*, translated by W. Trent and Arthur G. Holder (Liverpool: Liverpool University Press, 1999), xxx, 57.
67 Bede, *Commentary on Genesis*, edited by Charles W. Jones, II, vi 16, p. 108–119.
68 Bede, *Commentary on Genesis*, II vi 15–16, p. 107. What Bede says here follows the view of Augustine in *De Civitate Deo (City of God)* XV xxvi, edited by Dombart and A. Kalb, 48, 493–494.

69 Bede, *In Regnum Librum*, XXX questions, CCSL 119, p. 12.
70 Bede, *In Cantica Canticorum,* edited by David Hurst II in Cant 2 13–14, CCSL 119B, p. 224.
71 Richard Gameson, *The Role of Art in the Late Anglo-Saxon Church* (Oxford: Clarendon, 1995), plate 5b.
72 According a legend circulating at the time of Julian, Edith of Wilton (Queen and Abbess 1020–1075) commissioned a monk, Benno of Trier, to decorate a cruciform porch of her chapel, which she designed to house a relic: a nail of the original crucifixion. Benno was to paint Christ's passion on the wall exactly "as she had seen it in her heart" (surely a quite impossible task), and it seems this devotion to the passion, coupled with compassion for all people, increased until her death. See Andre Wilmot, "The Legend of St Edith in Prose and Verse", in *Analecta Bollandiana* 56 (1936): 5–101, 307.
73 Bernard of Clairvaux, *On the Song of Songs*, edited by Kilian Walsh and Irene Edmonds, (Kalamazoo, MI: Cistercian Publications, 1979), 111, 143–145.
74 "On Contemplating God", *The Works of William of St Thierry*, translated by Sr Penelope (Kalamazoo, MI: Cistercian Publications), I:38 and also 152–153.
75 Guieere d'Igny, *Liturgical Sermons*, translated by Monks of St Bernard Abbey, CF32 (Spencer: Cistercian, 1971). See the fourth sermon for Palm Sunday II 77. See also Caroline Walker Bynum, *Jesus as Mother: Studies in the Spirituality of the High Middle Ages* (Berkeley, CA: University of California Press), 121–122.
76 *The Works of Aelred of Rievaulx I Treatises on and Pastoral Prayer*, translated by M. P. McPherson (Spencer: Cistercian Studies, 1971), 73; cited in Bynum, *Jesus as Mother,* 123.
77 Bynum, *Jesus as Mother,* 132–133; see especially footnote 78.
78 Ruth Fulton, *From Judgement to Passion,* 422.
79 Bynum, *Jesus as Mother,* 162.
80 Karma Lochrie, *Mystical Acts, Queer Tendencies in Constructing Medieval Sexuality,* edited by Karma Lochrie and James A. Schultz (Minneapolis: University of Minnesota Press, 1997), 180–200; see particularly page 182.
81 For a useful history of the medieval and modern developments in this devotion, see Josef Stierli, "Devotion to the Sacred Heart from the End of Patristic Times down to St Margret Mary", in *Heart of the Saviour,* edited by Josef Sterli (New York: Herder, 1957), 59–130. See also K. Richstatter, *Medieval Devotions to the Sacred Heart* (London: Burns and Oates, 1925). The illustrations in Richstatter's

book from a number of medieval sources provide a useful visual compliment to the text of this chapter.

82 *The Works of Bonaventure*, translated by Jose de Vinck Patterson (St Anthony Guild, 1960), 95–144, 145–206. See especially page 128. Many of the key points of Bonaventure's proposal survive to this day in the Three Lessons of the Divine Office (Breviary) for the Third Nocturn of the Feast of the Sacred Heart.

83 "The Mystical Vine", in *The Works of Bonaventure*, translated by de Vinck, 155.

84 *The Exemplar: Life and Writings of Blessed Henry Suso*, translated by M. Ann Edward (Dubuque Priory: 1962), ch. 4, "He Brands the Name of Jesus on His Heart". See also pages 13–14. There is a no-doubt apocryphal story that "one day, as Henry Suso was re-carving the name of Jesus on his chest he happened to notice a puppy playing nearby. Seeing the little dog amusing itself with a dirty cloth gave the friar an epiphany. Suso realised that redemption is granted not to those who mortify the flesh—for to do so is merely to glorify oneself. Rather, one shows love for God by living in grace, simplicity and sportive celebration of the world. Like Dogs. Those who have seen dogs in action may well demur". Stuart Jefferies, "Happy as Lassie: A Review of Mark Alizart Dogs" *Polity*, 120, in *The Spectator Magazine: Arts and Books* (5 October 2019), 48.

85 For more on Suso's spiritual marriage and alternating gender roles, see Jager, *Book of the Heart*, 97–102.

86 On Rupert of Deutz's supposed spiritual pregnancy, see Fulton, *From Judgement to Passion*, 310–313.

87 "The Soul's Love-Book", in *The Exemplar II*, 344–349; see particularly 348.

88 Stierli, Richstatter, and Karl Rahner are all male, and many of those whom they cite in their works as having a special devotion to the Sacred Heart of other wounds are male too. See for example the names in the bibliography of Sterli's *Heart of the Saviour*. Although some female devotees are also mentioned, their unique contributions and their influence are marginalised. They are inadequately acknowledged and described. In more recent years, however, an increased concentration on female mystics has developed, and this serves to correct the balance, even if some are more than a little lurid and apparently designed to arouse in their interpretations.

89 Bynum, *Jesus as Mother*, ch. 5, "Women Mystics in the Thirteenth Century: The Case of the Nuns of Helfta", 170–260.

90 Hidegard of Bingen, *Symohonia*, 2nd ed., translated by Barbara Newman (Ithaca: Cornell University Press, 1998), 102–103.

91 The image is often reproduced. See, for example, Frances Beer, *Women and Mystical Experience in the Middle Ages* (Woodbridge: Boydell, 1992), 53.

92 See Gertrude Schiller, *Iconography in Christian Art Vol. 2, The Passion of Jesus Christ,* translated by Janet Seligman (Greenwich, CT: New York Graphic Society, 1971–1972), 371, 373, 432, 446–447, 527–529, 531.

93 See the introduction by Maximillian Marnau to *Gertrude of Helfta: The Herald of Divine Love,* translated by Margaret Winkworth (New York: Paulist, 1993), 34; Rosalynn Voaden, *All Girls Together: Gender and Value at Helfta in Medieval Women and Their Communities,* edited by Diane Watt (Cardiff: University of Wales Press, 1997), 72–91.

94 Some of the imagery here is surely close to the imagery used by Julian in the seventh and eight Showings. On Mecthild, see Mechthild von Magdeburg, *Das Fliessende Licht der Gottheit,* edited and translated by Margot Scmidt (Stutgart: Bad Cannstatt), 14. See in its English, translation by Shelia Hughes, in Emile Zum Brunn and Georgette Epiney-Burgard, *Women Mystics in Medieval Europe* (New York: Paragon House, 1989), 57.

95 Gertrude, *Herald,* translated by Barratt, Book 3, ch. 18, 72. See also Book 3, ch. 15, "The Tree of Love", 59–61.

96 Gertrude, *Herald,* Book 2, ch. 10, 128.

97 Gertrude, *Herald,* Book 2, ch. 9, 124–125.

98 Gertrude, *Herald,* Book 1, ch. 3, 47.

99 Gertrude, *Herald,* Book 3, ch. 26, 95; ch. 30, 102.

100 Like Julian, although Gertrude is fully intimate with Christ as lover, she also venerates him as Sovereign, Lord, and Judge. For more on this and how Gertrude forms a transition point from early medieval "tough" piety to the "gentle" piety of the late fourteenth century and especially that of Julian, see Bynum, *Jesus as Mother,* 187–190 The interplay of loving intimacy and the majesty of the sovereignty of God is central to the theology of Teresa of Avila; see my *How to See a Vision.*

101 Gertrude, *Herald,* Book 2, ch. 21, 168.

102 For an illustration of this, see Michael Camille, *The Medieval Art of Love* (New York: Harry N. Abrams, 1998), 58.

103 See Paul Lachance, ed., *Angela Foligno Complete Works* (New York: Paulist, 1993). 176. "At times it seems to my soul that it enters Christ's side, and this is a source of great joy and delight; it is indeed such a joyful experience to move into Christ's side that in no way can I express it or put it into words." We should

note here the similarity of Angela's paralysis of the limbs, her wish for death, and her desire to suffer with Christ with that of Julian.

104 Raymond of Capua, *The Life of Catherine of Sienna*, translated by Conleth Kearns (Wilmington: Michael Glazier, 1980). Quoted by Carolyn Walker Bynum, *Holy Feast and Holy Fast: The Significance of Food for Medieval Women* (Berkeley, CA: University of California Press, 1987), 172; and by Lochrie, *Mystical Acts, Queer Tendencies*, 188.See also Catherine of Sienna, *The Dialogue*, translated and with an introduction by Suzanne Noffke, with a preface by Giuliana Cavallini (New York: Paulist, 1980).

105 Flora Lewes, "The Wound in Christ's Side and the Instruments of Passion: Gendered Experience and Response", in *Women and the Book: Assessing the Visual Evidence*, edited by Leslie Smith and Jane H. M. Tatlor (London: The British Library, 1996), 204–229.

106 Lewes, *Wound*, 214–216. For the wound as vulva, see Lochrie, *Mystical Acts, Queer Tendencies*, 189–192 and figures 9.1 and 9.2.

107 Voaden, *All Girls Together*, 74, 85.

108 For example, Bede associates the blood of the Passion with the red berries of a pomegranate and cinnamon. These are references to the Song of Songs 4:3 and 4:4, respectively. See Bede, *In Cantica Canticorum*, edited by D. Hurst, 119B, 248.

109 Bonaventure, *The Mystical Vine*, ch. 15, "On the Red and Ardent Roase in General"; ch. 16, "On the Rose of Love"; ch. 17, "On the Rose of the Passion", 186–191, 200. Behold how the crimsoned Jesus blossomed forth the rose.

110 Hamburger, *Nuns as Artists*, ch. 2, "The Sweet Rose of Sorrow", 63–100.

111 Hamburger, *The Visual and the Visionary*, 139. This extremely gory drawing is shown in full colour in Hamburger, *Nuns as Artists*, plate 1, following page 134.

112 For an insightful analysis of Hamburger's book, see Caroline Walker Bynum's review in *History of Religions* 38 (1999): 407.

113 The gashed heart, usually surrounded with a ring of thorns and topped by a small cross, was a common emblem painted into Books of Hours and prayer books and even sewn on clothing. See again Hamburger, *Nuns as Artists*, figs. 77 and 78, 118–119.

114 Hamburger, *Nuns as Artists*, 116, and colour plate 10.

115 Versions and so-called translations of Julian's work abound. One of the most popular is Julian of Norwich, *Revelations of Divine Love*, translated by Elizabeth Spearing (Penguin, 1998). Many Julian scholars regard the Middle English

version in Edmund College and James Walsh, "A Book of Showings to the Anchoress Julian of Norwich", *Studies and Texts* 35 (1978) as the critical edition. Here, for convenience I have used Spearing, but later I will use other versions as indicated in their place. For those who wish to take their reading beyond Spearing, but perhaps not as far as reading Middle English, I recommend Julian of Norwich, *Showing of Love*, translated by Julian Bolton Holloway (Collegeville, MN: Liturgical Press, 2003); Julian of Norwich, *Revelation of Divine Love*, translated by Grace Warrack and modernised by Yolande Clark, with an introduction by A. N. Wilson (London 2017).

116 Julian Long Text 12, 59–60; cf. Short Text 8, 13.
117 Julian Long Text 24, 76; cf. Short Text 13, 20.
118 Julian Short Text 1, 125.
119 Julian: Short Text 1, 126.
120 Julian Short Text 1, 126.
121 In the Long Text 3, 179, Julian writes that this occurred on the third night.
122 Julian Short Text 1, 127.
123 That Julian was a universalist is much disputed, although personally I think there is much evidence to show that she was. For more on the notion of universal salvation generally, see George Macdonald, ed., *All Shall Be Well: Explorations in Universalism and Christian Theology from Origin to Moltmann* (Cambridge: James Clark & Co., 2011).
124 Veronica Mary Rolf has made great efforts to reconstruct it in her *Julian's Gospel: Illuminating the Life and Revelations of Julian of Norwich* (New York: Orbis Books Maryknoll, 2013), 15–194. All such attempts are, and must remain, largely a matter of fictional speculation.
125 Maria R. Lichtmann, *"God Fulifilled My Bodye": Body Self and God in Julian of Norwich in Gender and Text in the Later Middle Ages*, edited by Jane Chance (Gainesville, FL: University Press of Florida, 1996), 263–270.
126 *Anchoritic Spirituality: Ancrene Wisse and Associated Works*, translated and with an introduction by Anne Savage and Nicholas Walsh, with a preface by Benedicta Ward (New York: Paulist Press, 1991).
127 Ibid.
128 At least, we have no sources, autobiographical or other, to show that Julian did. Caroline Walker Bynum, *Holy Feast and Holy Fast: The Religious Significance of Food to Medieval Women* (Berkeley, CA: University of California Press, 1987).
129 Julian Short Text 2, 128.

130 Julian of Norwich, *Showings*, edited and translated by College and Walsh (New York: Paulist, 1978), 22.

131 Throughout this section, it may be well to have in mind 2 Timothy 2:12, "If we endure with him we shall also reign with him."

132 Unless otherwise stated, my textual references are to the Long Text.

133 Julian Long Text 15, 204.

134 Julian Long Text 15, 204.

135 Julian: Long Text 15, 205.

136 Julian of Norwich, *Showings*, edited and translated by College and Walsh, 43.

137 The Short Text renders this somewhat differently: "in my reason I was answered that despair is greater, for that is a spiritual pain. But there is no greater pain than this: how could I suffer greater pain than to see him who is my whole life, all my bliss and all my joy suffer?" (Julian Short Text 10, 142). Two things are noteworthy here. First, this is a clear instance of Julian's distinction between physical and spiritual pain. Second, this distinction is omitted in the passage in the Long Text which is quoted.

138 Julian Long Text 7, 209.

139 Julian Long Text 18, 210. This sharing of pain and its theological implications for the contemporary Church formed a central theme of my lecture to the Julian Festival Norwich 2019, which used material from my *How to See a Vision: Contemplative Ethics in Julian of Norwich and Teresa of Avila* (Bloomington, IN: AuthorHouse, 2013).

140 Julian Long Text 18, 210–211.

141 Julian Long Text 18 210.

142 Julian Long Text 19, 212.

143 Julian Long Text 19 212.

144 Julian Long Text 20, 213–214.

145 Julian Long Text 20, 214.

146 I am grateful to Fr Luke Penkett for his deep and prayerful wisdom on the nature of true compassion during our many conversations on the point at the meetings of the Friends and Companions of Julian, held twice each year in Norwich. His book, Touched by God's Spirit: How Merton, Van Gough, Vanier and Rembrandt Influenced Henri Nouwen's Heart of Compassion (London: DLT, 2019), is a masterly, much-needed, and perhaps unique contribution to the theology of compassion and suffering.

147 Cohen, *The Modulated Scream*, 15.

148 Julian Long Text 19, 211–212.
149 It is this link between the soul and the senses that accounts for the traditional idea, which still lingers in some quarters, that there is a direct relationship between pain and sickness as a punishment for the "poor" state of health (sin) in the soul. See the problem of the apportionment of blame in this book's appendix.
150 Ricoeur 1971a, 148.
151 Bultmann 1985, 246.
152 Again, I am grateful to Fr Luke Penkett for this suggestion as to what Julian's illness might have been. Although he is not medically trained, he is clear that either or both of these illnesses would certainly account for Julian's complaint of shortness of breath and intolerable pain.
153 Nicene Creed.
154 College and Walsh 1978a, 44
155 Julian Long Text 17, 209.
156 Sister Elizabeth Obbard, *A Revelation of Divine Love in the 16 Showings of Julian of Norwich for Everyone* (London 2018).
157 I argue it is for this reason that Julian places so much emphasis on her age at the start of her texts. She tells us very precisely that at the time of the Showings she was thirty and one-half years old. In medieval Europe, such an age marked a woman at the very height of her maturity and adulthood. Moreover, in Judaism, thirty and one-half years old had a special resonance. It told of her having reached the highest point of her spiritual wisdom and authority. That Julian makes such a point of her precise age, combined with her well-known knowledge of Hebrew to the extent that she is able to correct the Hebrew of the Vulgate, leads me to suspect that Julian, or at least her ancestors, may have been *conversos* in much the same way, and perhaps for similar reasons, as the family St Theresa of Avila.
158 Anne Hunsaker Hawkins, "A Change of Heart: The Paradigm of Regeneration in Medical and Religious Narrative", in *Perspectives in Biology and Medicine* 33, no. 4 (Summer 1990): 547–559. See especially page 547.
159 College and Walsh 1978a, 44; my emphasis added throughout.
160 Obbard, 27.
161 For a description of these "two" journeys and how they are connected, see Leichmann 1996, 269–270.